Julien de Narfon

Pope Leo XIII

His Life And Work

Julien de Narfon

Pope Leo XIII
His Life And Work

ISBN/EAN: 9783337248048

Printed in Europe, USA, Canada, Australia, Japan

Cover: Foto ©Lupo / pixelio.de

More available books at **www.hansebooks.com**

POPE LEO XIII

Frontispiece.   Pope Leo XIII.

POPE LEO XIII

HIS LIFE AND WORK

By JULIEN DE NARFON

TRANSLATED FROM THE FRENCH BY

G. A. RAPER

WITH NUMEROUS ILLUSTRATIONS AND PORTRAITS

LONDON: CHAPMAN & HALL, Ld.
1899

RICHARD CLAY & SONS, LIMITED,
LONDON & BUNGAY.

CONTENTS

PART I

CHAPTER I

THE POPE'S EARLY LIFE

CHAPTER II

SCHOOL DAYS

CHAPTER III

STUDENT DAYS IN ROME

CHAPTER IV

THE PRELACY

PART II

CHAPTER I

ELECTION AND CORONATION

CHAPTER II

THE VATICAN

CHAPTER III

THE PAPAL FAMILY

CHAPTER IV

THE POPE'S DAILY LIFE

CHAPTER V

A POLITICAL POPE

CHAPTER VI

THE POPE AND THE PRESS

CHAPTER VII

THE POPE AS WRITER AND POET

CHAPTER VIII

THE POPE AND THE AMERICAN MOVEMENT

CHAPTER IX

THE FUTURE POPE

LIST OF ILLUSTRATIONS

POPE LEO XIII

PART I

CHAPTER I

Carpineto—The Pecci family and their home—The Pope's birth and childhood.

THE cradle of Leo XIII was placed by Providence in Carpineto, an ancient town of the Volscians. The name of the place signifies an elm-forest, and no doubt the mountain on which the town stands was originally covered with trees of this kind. The traveller who makes his way from Rome to Carpineto by rail must leave the train at Segui. Here he will find a prehistoric diligence which will manage to convey him to his journey's end in about three hours; but the contemplation of the wonderful Alpine panorama will render him oblivious to fatigue and the flight of time.

The Carpineto houses, built in an ancient but unmistakably pure style of architecture, and many of them distinguished by armorial bearings, are grouped around two hills. On the higher stand the family mansion of the Pecci, and the Church of St. Leo, a Grecian temple for which the

B

Carpinetans are indebted to their illustrious fellow-citizen.
The Pope has, moreover, restored all the churches in Carpineto, and has done his utmost to provide for the bodily
needs of his townsmen by building, first of all, a men's
hospital placed under the management of the Brotherhood
of Mercy, a women's hospital and an almshouse conducted
by the Ladies of the Holy Sacrament, and finally two large
public fountains.

On one of these fountains, which stands in the open space
opposite the church, is the following inscription :—

"LEO XIII P. M.

AQUAM SALUBERRIMI HAUSTUS

E MONTIBUS LEPINIS

PERDUCENDAM CURAVIT

AN. SAC. PRINC. X."[1]

The following delightful lines from the Pope's pen are
also engraved on the fountain :—

"Fons ego decurrens, nitidis argenteus undis
Quem cupide irriguum florea prata bibant ;
At non prata bibent, cives, me florea ; vestras
Gratius est largo spargere rore domos."[2]

On the second fountain, which stands in front of the
Pecci mansion, we find another Papal evocation of the Muse.
Both structures bear the Pontifical arms.

[1] The Sovereign Pontiff Leo XIII caused this most salubrious water
from the Lepini mountains to be brought hither, in the tenth year of
his Pontificate.

[2] Spring whose silvery waters the flowery meadows eagerly seek to
drink ; not their thirst, O citizens, do I desire to assuage, but rather
to abundantly supply your dwellings.

The Carpineto peasant is poor, but supports his poverty courageously. Maize bread is his only food when the crops prove a failure. The Carpinetans have preserved intact the simple faith of their fathers. All the ancient pious customs of the locality are carefully observed. For instance, at harvest time every man goes at nightfall to the parish church with a sheaf of wheat from the field on which he has toiled since sunrise, and places his offering at the foot of the Virgin's altar, while the vaulted roof resounds to the time - honoured shout of praise, *Viva Maria! Viva la Madonna!*

The Pecci mansion at Carpineto.

The Pecci family sprang from Cortona, and was established at the beginning of the fourteenth century at Sienna, from which town it removed to Carpineto. Many distinguished politicians and diplomatists can be traced amongst the Pope's paternal ancestors. Paul Pecci, who flourished in the fifteenth century, was by turns Ambassador to Naples and a military commander holding the rank of general. Lelio

Pecci was Ambassador from the Republic of Sienna to the Court of Charles V. Giacomo Pecci was given the castle of Spoleto by Pope Martin V in recognition of his services. Giovanni Baptista Pecci, vicar-general of Anagni in the time of Clement XIII, Colonel Antonio Pecci, Ferdinando Pecci the eminent jurist and friend of Benedict XIV, Joseph Pecci the confidant of Pius VI and Pius VII, and many other distinguished members of the family may be cited. More than this, the Pecci have contributed two saints to the calendar—the blessed Pietro Pecci, founder of the Order of the Hermits of St. Jerome, and the blessed Margherita Pecci, of the Servitors of Mary. Bernardini Pecci, a missionary in India, occupies an honoured place on the Jesuit martyr-roll.

Count Ludovico Pecci, the Pope's father, had been given a colonel's commission by his feudal lord, Prince Aldobrandini Borghese, and was placed in command of the Baronial Militia raised by the Prince in the districts of Carpineto, Maenza, and Garignano. During the French invasion the Baronial Militia assumed the title of Civic Guard of the Volscian territory, though it does not appear that they became any more formidable in consequence. In 1809 Colonel Pecci was appointed Mayor of Carpineto by the French Government. In his double capacity as chief magistrate and Lord of the Manor he possessed very great influence, which he merited not only by his devotion to the public good, but by the stainless dignity of his life. Through his mother, Anna Prosperi Busi, who belonged to one of the twelve patrician families of Cori, a small town near Carpineto, the Pope is descended from the famous demagogue Cola di Rienzi. The august Pontiff has thus a few drops of revolutionary blood in his veins. An attempt has been made to explain his avowed tenderness for democracy by this distant consanguinity. The explanation is to be found easily enough in the Pope's own individuality without seeking for it in the operation of mysterious and uncertain laws which science will, perhaps, never be able to explain.

Seven children were born to Count Ludovico and Anna Prosperi Busi: Carlo (1793—1879), Anna Maria (1798—1870), Catarina (1800—1867), Giovanni Baptista (1802—1881), Giuseppe (1807—1890), Gioacchimo Vincenzo Raffaello Luigi (March 2, 1810), and Ferdinando (1816—1830). Thanks to Giovanni Baptista, who married, and left several sons, the Pecci will not die out with Leo XIII. One alone of Count Ludovico's children still survives, and from every part of the Catholic world prayer is offered without ceasing, that God may prolong to the utmost limits of old age the days of one so precious to His Church.

At the beginning of the nineteenth century, the family mansion—or the Pecci Palace, as it was afterwards called—was occupied by Colonel Ludovico and his wife. The palace, with its barred windows, has an austere and almost monastic appearance. A large modern stairway leads up to a massive double-swing door, adorned with bronze knockers bearing the Pecci arms. While left to his meditations in the salon, the visitor might almost imagine that the Pope in person was doing the honours of the old mansion, for the eye is irresistibly attracted by a full-length portrait of Leo XIII, clad in his

Pontifical robes. The noble and expressive countenance of the august original is admirably portrayed. The lips seem as if about to give utterance to words of greeting. Portraits of the Pope's ancestors next claim notice. Those of his Holiness' father and mother occupy the places of honour. Colonel Count Ludovico Pecci is represented powdered after the fashion of his time, and wearing a blue velvet coat braided with gold and faced with red. The buttons are stamped with the Pontifical tiara and keys. Countess Anna, who looks charming in her double-caped robe, cut open at the neck, and set off with trinkets and braiding, is painted with her right hand resting on her fan, the left hand holding the brim of her plumed hat. The nobility, the grace, the devotion, the love, and the legitimate pride expressed in the features of this patrician beauty, almost tempt one to salute her with the words uttered by the angel nineteen centuries ago to the Virgin chosen by God to be the mother of the Saviour—"Blessed art thou among women."

From the salon we may pass into "Monsignor's room." In this apartment, with its yellow furniture and hangings, Joachim Pecci has spent many hours, as we are informed by an inscription in abbreviated Latin, of which the following is a translation :—

"Stranger, in this chamber of his paternal abode, Leo XIII, prelate, delegate, bishop, and cardinal several times abode. Count Ludovico Pecci, in honour of his august uncle, caused it to be restored and gave it a renewed splendour, A.D. 1884."

In a plain frame, hanging close to the portrait of the blessed Marguerite Pecci, is the brief note in which Leo XIII sent his first apostolic benediction to his brothers, together with the announcement of his election to the Pontificate.

"*From the Vatican, February* 20, 1878.

"VERY DEAR BROTHERS,

"I have to tell you that at the election of this morning the Sacred College deigned to elevate my humble person to the chair of St. Peter. This is my first letter, and wishing the family all happiness, I send you the apostolic benediction with my love. Pray earnestly to God for me.

"LEO P. P. XIII."

Two other apartments in the Pecci Palace deserve special mention: the library and the room in which Leo XIII first saw the light. The library is a very large four-sided room with a table in the centre. The walls are lined with well-laden shelves, beneath which are cupboards. The largest of these cupboards, standing under the only window, contains the Pope's school copy-books and letters dating from his eighth year. Count Ludovico, the eldest of the three sons born to John Baptist Pecci, who died in 1882, guards these treasures with pious care, but is always ready to show them to properly recommended visitors whose love for the Pope may have induced them to make the pilgrimage to Carpineto. To all such visitors the Count extends a lordly hospitality. with a delightful simplicity peculiarly his own. The Pope's school-boy correspondence has been published at length by M. Boyer d'Agen in his book *The Youth of Leo XIII*, a work which is not only full of interesting facts, but is characterized by a charming and graceful style. We shall have frequent occasion to refer to this correspondence, wherein the future Pope, unconscious of his high destiny, lays bare the inmost

recesses of his mind in all candour and sincerity.   The other
apartment in the Pecci Palace calling specially for our attention
is now a perfect museum of family relics.   In the tall glass cases
are to be seen the Pope's sporting gun and white papal cassock,

Count Pecci, father of Leo XIII.

his cardinal's hat and that of his brother Joseph, side by side
with the brocaded robes and silken coats of dead-and-gone
Pecci.   On the 2nd March, 1810, he whose reign was destined
to become a pure and shining light in the firmament of the
Church, was born in this room.   A few minutes after the

happy event, Colonel Count Ludovico Pecci issued from the
Countess' chamber and presented the newly-born child to the
villagers, who, in accordance with custom, were assembled in
one of the salons of their lord's manor-house. From every

Countess Pecci, mother of Leo XIII.

throat burst the joyful cry, *Evviva ser Vincenzo Gioacchimo
Pecci!* and soon the shepherds with their flutes and pipes
announced far and wide the birth of the future Pope.

The child was baptized on the 4th March, the certificate
being drafted as follows:—

" In the year of our Lord 1810, on the fourth day of March, at the sixteenth hour (about ten o'clock in the morning), the Very Reverend Michael Catoni, canon of the most holy cathedral church of Anagni, baptized, by permission of the undersigned, a child, born two days before to the most illustrious lord and lady Ludovico Pecci and Anna Prosperi, residents in this parish of St. Nicholas (Carpineto), in the names of Vincent Joachim Raphael Louis. The sponsors were the most illustrious and most reverend Joachim Tosi, Bishop of Anagni, who appointed as his representative the reverend Hyacinth Canco Caporossi, from whom I have received his authority in due form ; and the most illustrious lady Candida Pecci Caldarozzi. In witness whereof I, Zephirin Cima, vicar of this parish," etc.

Mgr. Tosi, the Bishop of Anagni, had promised to baptize the infant, but was prevented from doing so, and had to confine himself to giving the child his own name, Joachim. The chapel of the palace, in which the baptism took place, is dedicated to a French saint, Vincent Ferrier. Hence the name Vincent (Vincenzino) given to the child at the request of the Countess. From his earliest years the future Pope was called Nino in the family circle. Until his mother's death he signed himself " Vincent," to which he subsequently added, for a time, Joachim. This latter name he eventually used alone until his elevation to the chair of St. Peter.

The disturbances due to the Revolution made considerable inroads into the wealth of the great landed proprietors, and the Pecci family fared no better than the majority of their neighbours. They were obliged to deny themselves to a considerable extent in order to provide for the education of the children, and especially of Joseph and Joachim. The Countess, however, was a woman of great intelligence and rare courage. She was, moreover, a genuine Christian. Instead of giving way to useless lamentations over the wickedness of humanity and the hardness of the times, she decided to have recourse to toil for the benefits denied to her by fortune. She saw nothing derogatory to her position in taking up the cultivation of silk-worms, and this lucrative industry afterwards made up the deficiency in the family finances caused by the education of the future Pope and Cardinal. Joseph and Joachim grew up under the vigilant eye of this incomparable mother. Writing to her brother-in-law Antony Pecci she says :—" Little Vincent can already walk alone. He finds his way all over the house. He has a passion for horses. Although he is hardly big enough to be seen, he gets astride of the chairs without holding on. Yesterday, when out with one of the servants, he insisted on leading your saddle-horse by the bridle to the fountain. He led the horse quite unaided, and we were in fits of laughter at hearing him admonish the horse with a ' Woa ' like a full-grown ostler." The child is father of the man, and it may not be too much to say that one of the most characteristic traits of the great Pope is discernible in the little boy who insisted on leading his uncle's horse, " all by himself."

Somewhat later than his brother Joseph, but nevertheless early in life, Joachim Pecci rejoiced his pious mother by giving signs, not only of a pronounced taste for study, but of a call towards religion. M. Boyer d'Agen relates that Count

Ludovico one day took the child for a walk, and pointed out
to him the spot on which Aquino was supposed to have stood,
and, a little further on, Monte Cassino.

"Yes," observed Joachim, "Aquino, where the learned
St. Thomas was born, and Monte Cassino, where he learnt
to read and write. Papa, shall we go there, and learn to
read and write like he did?"

From whom could Joachim Pecci have received at so
tender an age this sort of initiation to the cult of the
sanctified scholar, whom he was one day to call "the archimandrite of theologians," and of whose work he was one
day to compel acceptance by the entire Church—the colossal
and mysterious work in which the inspired monk seems to
exhaust the possibilities of human reason, and to penetrate
the mysteries of faith as far as the heart and mind of man
can carry him?

. Count Ludovico returned to the Pecci Palace somewhat
disappointed. Joachim's wish that he might learn to read
and write like the learned St. Thomas Aquinas, was quite
contrary to the Count's plans for the future of his dear
Nino.

"I wanted to make a general of him," the Count said sadly
to his wife.

"Well," replied the Countess, "you will make a Pope of
him."

Not long afterwards, the father and mother, overcoming
their repugnance to a separation from their children, decided
to send Joseph and Joachim to the college kept by the Jesuit
fathers at Viterbo. Nevertheless, Count Ludovico was still

far from pleased with the prospect of his favourite son taking holy orders.

"I can understand," he said, "that Joseph will never be anything more than a Jesuit, but I cannot reconcile myself to the idea that Joachim may come back to us a village *curé*."

To which the Countess, who held fast to her belief in her sons' vocation, rejoined :—

"Imagine that Joachim will be Pope and Joseph a Cardinal, and rest easy as to the future of our children."

The noble lady was perhaps less confident than she desired to appear. The health of her Vincenzino, who was to enter college at the October quarter, 1818, caused her considerable anxiety. At one period, indeed, she feared that her strength would not be equal to the new sacrifice required of her. "The separation," she wrote to Canon Gavellucci, her sons' first master, "is a great trial to me. Who knows whether I shall be able to endure it? Can it be that God will not give me courage?"

God gave her the courage she asked. Has not He destined the mother's heart to be, in the words of Father de Ravignan, "the accustomed place of grief"?

CHAPTER II

SCHOOL DAYS

In the Jesuit College—Father Ubaldini's predictions—Story of a tonsure—First Communion—A ten-year-old poet—Taking Orders—A mother's death.

THE boys supported the bitterness of separation better than their mother was able to do. As is well known, those unrivalled educationalists the Jesuits are skilled in the art of smoothing over the abrupt transition from family to school life. They are called Fathers, but they are in reality something more, for their ever-watchful tenderness rises, by a sort of permanent miracle, to the height of maternal love, and their schools are like large families. As early as October 6, Countess Anna was able to write as follows :—

"The letters I am beginning to receive from Viterbo are excellent. The boys are very happy, and the Fathers are satisfied with them. Consequently I have great hopes that they will be a comfort to me. They are now for the time being at a villa, a mile from Viterbo, and are playing to their hearts' content and eating well. I hope they will remain in good health and do themselves credit." This they did, as a letter written about this time to the Countess by Fathe

14

Ubaldini, the rector of the college, testifies:—"I well know how great is a mother's love, and I am not surprised to hear that the separation has been most painful to you. But you can take consolation in the thought that some day you will derive the purest joy and the most legitimate comfort from it, for so excellent are the natures of the two boys you have entrusted to me that I anticipate a great future for them. I

Country house of the Pecci at Carpineto.

love them much, because they are good, and are already bearing the fruits of a wisely directed education." The good Father could hardly have imagined that his prediction would be so completely fulfilled! Experience confirmed the favourable impression he had conceived. "Vincenzino," he wrote on April 9, 1820, "still behaves admirably, and is quite a little angel. Peppino is rather more lively, and is developing into a first-class scamp: not that I have any cause to complain of him, but he keeps me constantly on the alert, and makes me stand sentry in spite of myself."

"Scamps" have their good points. Educationalists worthy of the name find more in them than in those slower natures whose good qualities are rather of the passive type. This, in fact, was the opinion of Mgr. Dupanloup. "In a good education," wrote the illustrious Bishop of Orleans, "the pupil's very defects are used as a means of strengthening his character. Little by little these defects succumb to whatever good qualities there may be, and in the long run these qualities, thanks to the effort they have been called upon to make, develop into virtues." Peppino demonstrated the soundness of this theory by becoming the model of ecclesiastics and an honour to the Senate of the Church.

Vincenzino had barely entered his eleventh year when his mother, who desired above all things that her children should consecrate themselves to God, implored Mgr. Carmine Lolli, the Papal delegate at Viterbo, to confer the tonsure upon them.

"Dear Monsignor," she wrote, "permit me to make one humble request to you. I wish to place my two boys in the Church, and to start them on their ecclesiastical career. If, later on, they do not wish to continue in this path, they will be at full liberty to follow their own inclinations. My husband asks me to say that it would give him great pleasure for them to accept the tonsure. Will you not give this satisfaction to their father and mother?" (March 17, 1821.)

Singularly enough, Mgr. Lolli felt no surprise at a proposal which might have been considered at least premature

Far from it: he immediately sympathized with the Countess' wish. Writing on the 25th March, he says :—

" I think your idea excellent. You must ask the Bishop of Anagni for the letters dismissory, so that Nino and Peppino may be included in his diocese. If you will send me these documents I will manage the rest."

The Bishop of Anagni was no more surprised at the request than the Pope's delegate at Viterbo had been. Before three weeks had elapsed Mgr. Lolli was in possession of the required documents. Nothing more remained to be done except the slight formality of mentioning the matter to the parties interested, and asking for their consent.

" To-morrow," wrote Mgr. Lolli on the 22nd April, "Father Ubaldini, Father Bonelli and the two boys will be here to dinner. I will take advantage of the opportunity to urge the children to set to work at once to learn the little catechism in which they will be examined before they are granted the tonsure."

The dinner took place, but the result was not in accordance with the wishes of Monsignor the delegate. The letter in which he relates his discomfiture to the Countess is very curious :—

"The boys came to spend the second Easter festival here. Before they were taken to my official residence by Fathers Ubaldini and Bonelli, the good Bishop of Viterbo happened to pay me a visit. He came just at the right time, and I begged him to be good enough to tonsure the children. With the utmost kindness he offered to do so at once. It also happened by good fortune your sons entered the room at this juncture. I again told them of their parents' wish, but they

frankly replied that such was not their will, and that they had
already expressed their views on the matter to Father
Ubaldini." (May 1, 1821.)

Thus it appears that the Bishop of Viterbo was no more
surprised than Mgr. Lolli or the Bishop of Anagni at the
proposal to tonsure two children whose consent was, to
say the least, doubtful. This glimpse at ecclesiastical ways
on the other side of the Alps is a curious one.

In any case, Nino and Peppino had distinctly refused to
allow themselves to be tonsured. "Such was not their
will." The duty of reporting their refusal to the Countess
devolved upon Nino. He accomplished it with a variety
of epistolary precautions, so as to make his mother's disap-
pointment as light as possible.

"Yesterday," he wrote, "Monsignor the delegate had us
to dinner with Father Ubaldini and his companion. After
dinner he told us that in his view we ought to take the tonsure.
This somewhat surprised us, and we have been unable to
decide in the affirmative; nevertheless, we have not failed to
pray to the Lord and the Holy Virgin that we may be
led to do the will of God. We hope that you will also
ask for guidance on the matter, and with more success
than we can attain."

In the meantime Monsignor the delegate was racking his
brains to discover a reason for the boys' unexpected resistance
to their mother's desire.

"Nino and Peppino," he writes, "are evidently afraid to
be the only boys in the school to wear the priestly *collare* and
capello, and of being called 'parsons' by their playmates, but

General view of Carpineto.

everything will be put right at your next visit. You will be satisfied with your sons; their conduct is excellent and their health is still better. In the meantime do not fail, when you write, to urge them to reflect how necessary it is that there should be clerics in the Pecci family, in view of the benefices and prebends to which their descent gives them a claim."

The last part of this letter is hardly to my taste. No doubt the Italian way of regarding these matters differs from the French. I am also fully convinced that when Vincent Joachim Pecci finally gave way to the urgent representations of his mother, and offered his young brow to the Bishop of Viterbo's golden scissors, he was not yielding to purely human considerations. Father Ubaldini, who was an excellent judge, said of him :—"Joachim Vincent is a very good boy and fills me with satisfaction. He is really a little angel." The boy's letters display the sincerest piety. Here is a specimen :—

> *"Viterbo, November* 11, 1821.
>
> "MADAME AND VERY DEAR MOTHER,
>
> "Your presents have pleased both me and my brother very much. This mark of your attachment can only make us strengthen our own for you, as it is our duty to do, in proportion to your desire. Yes, we will do this, but we need your prayers to help us to give you full satisfaction, so grant us those prayers. For some time you have kept us in hope that you would come and embrace us, but the moment has not yet arrived. Imagine how sad your absence makes us. Images of saints, whoever they may be, will always be pleasing to us, but the prettier they are the more we shall like them. Remember us to papa and others. Give me your blessing, and let me kiss your hands with tender affection, and sign myself
>
> "Your most affectionate son,
>
> "VINCENT."

Vincenzino had already received his first communion on
the 21st June of the same year, the fête-day of St. Louis of
Gonzaga. Precocious poet as he was, he celebrated the
occasion by attempting to compose a Latin sonnet in honour
of the young saint whom successive generations of pupils in
the Jesuits' colleges are taught to hail as one of the greatest

Library of the Pecci Palace, Carpineto.

ornaments of the illustrious company. For many years this
sonnet was hidden among the archives of the Pecci Palace.
A little more than two years ago it was brought to light, and
placed in the Pope's hands on the 22nd June, 1896, exactly
seventy-five years after it was written. Leo XIII slowly
perused the verses, half effaced by time, but nevertheless

bright with the purest souvenirs of his youth. It is said that when the Pope at length raised his eyes from the time-stained paper, a big tear fell upon it—a priceless tear,

but yet, perhaps, less precious in the sight of God than the angelic smile of the youthful communicant.

Father Leonard Giribaldi was Joachim's instructor in Latin and Italian. Latin verses were then in favour, and the future Pope practised his pen *a teneris unguiculis*, in the language of Virgil. In reply to repeated requests, his mother sent him a *Regia Parnassi*, for which he thanked her in

Nephew and niece of Leo XIII in the garden at Carpineto.

verse, and the delighted mother rewarded her poet by sending him, through Monsignor the assistant legate, a basket of cakes and two crowns. Not long after this eleven-year-old poet had composed his sonnet in honour of St.

Louis of Gonzaga, he favoured the Reverend Father Vincent Pavoni, the provincial head of the Jesuits, with the following couplets :—

> " Nomine Vincenti quo tu, Pavone, vocaris
>   Parvulus atque infans Peccius ipse vocor.
> Quas es virtutes magnas, Pavone, secutus,
>   O ! utinam possim Peccius ipse sequi ! "[1]

The compliment is not at all badly expressed. It certainly displays very considerable aptitude. Though the school-boy's poetic attempts can hardly be held up to *dilettanti* as masterpieces, they are none the less full of promise. Even thus does the tender blossom precede the luscious fruit.

In spite of his marked predilection for Latin verses, Joachim by no means neglected the other branches of a classical education. Writing to the Countess on the 27th August, 1822, Mgr. Lolli says :—" On Saturday I presided at a philosophical dissertation, dedicated to his Eminence, Cardinal Galeffi, the Bishop of Viterbo, and held in the Jesuits' church. On the same occasion it fell to my lot to distribute the prizes to the young scholars of this institution. It gave me very great pleasure to award the first prize for rhetoric to our Peppino, and the second prize for the humanities to our Vincenzino. Peppino's prize is a big silver medal, and Vincenzino's a smaller medal, also silver. Their names are recorded on the enclosed certificate. I send you this news so that the progress of your children may rejoice your

---

[1] The name of Vincent which thou, Pavoni, bearest, is also that bestowed on me, Pecci, a little child. Those great virtues which thou, Pavoni, practisest, may I, Pecci, also practise !

heart, and enable you to increase their father's pride in them."

Soon after the receipt of this letter the Countess began to suffer from the disease which was to put an end to her life. From this period Joachim's letters contain little but accounts of the alternate hope and despair excited in his breast by the contradictory accounts of his beloved mother's health. "The incessant attacks of fever from which mamma suffers every day," he writes to his uncle Antony Pecci, "are the cause of great suffering to her and to all the family, especially ourselves. We expected to see her back again this month (May 1824), as she had promised us to do if she were better. But my father's letter, thank God, tells us the doctors consider her illness has now reached its height, and that it can be overcome by quinine. Nevertheless, we steadfastly pray the most Holy Virgin that our mamma's health may return." The illness was, in fact, at its height, but quinine was powerless against it. Under the doctors' orders the Countess had consented to leave Carpineto and take up her abode in the Muti Palace at Rome, the residence of her brother-in-law, Antony Pecci. Immediately after her arrival she became so much worse that all hope of her recovery was abandoned, and her children were hastily summoned to her bedside. She survived a month longer, Providence having vouchsafed this pious mother one last consolation before the angel of death should summon her from the uncertainty and misery of this lower world. In her last letter, written to her husband on the 5th July, she says :—"I made Joachim put on the priest's cassock and mantle. The three-cornered hat suits him admirably. He hesitated at first, but, like the good boy he is, he appeared very glad afterwards. Peppino would have put on clerical garb too, but he said it would be an unnecessary expense for us, as he has resolved to be a Jesuit. His acts are really those of a St. Louis. He hopes to enter upon his novitiate in October, after he has seen you all." Thus was it permitted to this noble woman to see, as through a glass darkly, the fulfilment of her dream. It may be that, in that terrible and mysterious moment before the entrance of the soul into eternity, God, in His infinite goodness, deigned to soothe the terrors of this pure mind with a revelation of the glorious destiny awaiting the son who knelt sobbing at her death-bed.

Anne Frances Pecci died August 5, 1824. Her eyes were closed by Joachim. Years afterwards, in recalling the memory of her death, he described her as " the benefactress of the poor, a peerless mother, and a woman of all the ancient virtues." The Countess lies buried in the church of the Stimmate, at Rome. The epitaph engraved on her tomb is as follows :—

" Here lies Anne Prosperi, mother of the poor, most affectionate to her children, born at Cori, a saintly woman, gentle and generous. After an exemplary fulfilment of all the duties of a mother, she died, lamented by every honest heart, during the nones of August, MDCCCXXIV. She lived 51 years 7 months and 11 days, in sweet companionship with those around her. Ludovico Pecci and her afflicted children raised this monument to this unique and incomparable woman. Peace be unto thee, pure soul."

CHAPTER III

STUDENT DAYS IN ROME

A new Gregory of Nazianza—The first oration—The 1829 Conclave—Curious sketch of a new Pope by a future Pope—The Reverend
Joachim Pecci as sportsman—Father Salvagni—First public thesis—
The 1831 Conclave—The Revolution—Reporter and diplomatist—A
poet on death—The Arcadian shepherd.

In November 1824 Joachim entered the Roman College, in
which there were then fourteen hundred pupils. He remained
there seven years, studying literature, science, philosophy,
and theology with an unflagging ardour to which all his
masters and fellow-students bear witness. His teachers of
rhetoric were Fathers Minimi and Bonvicini, and he obtained
the first prize both for orations and Latin verses. Count
Antony Pecci had undertaken to reward the success of a
nephew of whom he was justly proud, and, to judge by the
following letter to his brother Charles, Joachim took care
not to forget his generous uncle's promise :—

"As to the prizes my poor efforts have obtained for me,
not without some trouble, you would please me very much
by mentioning them to papa and particularly to Uncle
Antony, who promised me a watch, on his word of honour!!!"

27

This letter was dated from Maenza, where Joachim was
spending the holidays with another brother, John Baptist.
The month of October following brought him back to Rome,
where he set to work again with passionate energy. For
two whole months his brothers heard nothing from him. He
was entirely absorbed in study. That year and the two

following years he
took first prizes in
logic, metaphysics,
moral philosophy,
mathematics, physics
and chemistry. As
one of the fellow-
students remarked of
him in the *Civiltà
Cattolica* :—" During
his studies in Rome
he had neither society
nor amusement. His
desk was his world,
scientific investiga-
tion his paradise."

Inscription in the church of St. Leo, at Carpineto,
engraved by Leo XIII when a young priest.

" As Basil and
Gregory of Nazianza did before him," says the Abbé Bertrin
in his work *Great Catholics,* " the only roads he knew
were those that led to church and school." The distinguished Professor of the Catholic Institute in Paris might
have added, that there was one way to lure Joachim Pecci
out of these chosen paths. All that was necessary was

Bedroom of Leo XIII in the Pecci Palace at Carpineto.

to put him on the track of some rare book. "I thank you
infinitely," he writes to his father (April 18, 1827), "for the
money you have been so good as to send me. Like what
I have had from you before, it will not be used for anything
except the purchase of some good book. I may mention
that my little library has been increased by about twenty
volumes during the year."

It may be remembered that from his earliest childhood
Joachim displayed a sort of instinctive admiration for St.
Thomas Aquinas. At the very beginning of his theological
studies he gave further proofs of this admiration, now all the
stronger for being fortified by reason. He wrote in these
terms to his brother Charles, November 12, 1828 :—

"I write to ask you to do me the favour of sending me as soon as
possible, on the first opportunity you have, St. Thomas Aquinas'
Theological Burden. You will find it in our little study, on the theology
shelf. If you should also happen to find some book on dogmatic—not
moral—theology, I should be very glad if you would send it to me at
your convenience. St. Thomas, however, I should like to have at once.
He is the archimandrite of theologians."

The Professor of Dogma at the Roman College at that
time was the celebrated Father Perrone. The Scripture
Professor was Father Patrizzi, who, many years afterwards,
had the joy of being present at the elevation of his pupil to
the Pontificate. These two eminent ecclesiastics greatly
esteemed Joachim Pecci, and it was, moreover, his rare good
fortune to have none but friends among his fellow-students.
His superiority was, moreover, so evident that he was
unanimously chosen to head the deputation sent by the
students of the Roman College to Leo XII on the occasion

of the jubilee granted by that Pope to the Catholic world.
It fell to Joachim Pecci to address the Sovereign Pontiff in
the language of Cicero.   His speech delighted the venerable
Pope, and would certainly have had some influence on
Joachim's future had Leo XII lived long enough to give
practical effect to the special favour with which he deigned
to honour the young orator.   The Pope, however, was recalled to God on the 10th February, 1829.   His successor,
Francesco Severio Castiglioni, who reigned as Pius VIII,
was elected on the 31st March.   Joachim kept his family
informed of the smallest details of the Conclave in a series
of letters which would have done credit to a "special
correspondent."   This is how he described the circumstances
of the election, in a letter to his brother John Baptist :—

    " Nobody would have believed that such an event could
take place on Tuesday, March 31.   On Sunday the 29th rain
began to fall, and continued throughout the day and Monday.
On Tuesday it increased to such an extent that the streets
were perfect lakes.   The fact that the Tiber nearly over-
flowed caused no surprise.   How could a Pope be expected
in such weather ?

            *   *   *   *   *   *

    " As usual, popular opinion is divided into two currents—
those who are pleased with the new Pope and those who are
not.   The politicians, who invariably doubt the possibility of
good organization in the Papal States, are dissatisfied ; the
learned extol the new Pope's doctrines and his great knowledge.   The people, who are always foolish and unstable,
congratulate themselves on a piece of good fortune from

which they may never derive any benefit. On the whole, however, the Pope is popular. His neck is askew, and he walks as if he were dancing."

Hitherto we have not discovered any traces of irony in Joachim Pecci's character, but here we find a new trait in our hero's complex personality. In a few lines he hits off the professionally sceptical politicians, the learned men whose interest in the new Pope is excited solely by his erudition, and the populace, that big, simple, credulous child, perpetually disappointing its hunger and thirst for happiness by constantly renewed illusions. It does not seem that the nineteen-year-old philosopher who wrote the foregoing lines had many illusions of his own to lose.

The letter ends as follows:—

"I believe I once heard that the Pope stayed at our house at Carpineto when he was Vicar-General under Mgr. Devoti, Bishop of Anagni. If this were a fact, it would be a favourable opportunity to record so happy an event on the walls of our house. Find out if this is so; papa would certainly remember it. Is he still fond of news? If so, please send him these gossiping letters of mine without delay."

We shall soon find traces of a very different kind of thought in Joachim's correspondence. The Papal election does not absorb his attention to such an extent as to make him forget his plans for his annual holiday. These plans are the same, year after year. He is as passionately fond of shooting as he is in love with study, and the passion is no less exclusive than the love. Shooting is thus his only

D

holiday amusement, just as study is his sole object throughout
the scholastic year.   He writes to his brother John Baptist
from Rome, September 12 :—

"Do you not think it would be as well to send me the
gun-lock I used last October, before I return to Carpineto ?
It seemed to me rather defective.   I will have it cleaned and
put in good order."

Jesuits' College at Viterbo, where Leo XIII was educated.

Six days
afterwards he
wrote :—

"Many thanks
for so quickly
sending me the
gun-lock. I shall
have it cleaned
by the burnisher,
as it seems rather
rusty and stiff.
Thanks for your
warning against
gunsmiths ; they
certainly might
play us one of their tricks, such as palming off an inferior
gun on us instead of our own.   Thanks also for your
reminder to buy my stock of powder and lead here in
Rome, and to get the best quality as cheaply as possible.
This is just what I intended to do."

Some years ago M. Boyer d'Agen interviewed an old
inhabitant of Carpineto, "Father" Salvagni, who was usually

the witness of Joachim Pecci's sporting exploits. Old
Salvagni chattered readily about his souvenirs of half-a-
century before, but he complained that the Pope was no
longer the "jovial sportsman" of yore, and his dissatisfaction,
as conveyed to us by the author of *The Youth of Leo XIII*,
is full of contempt for mere grandeur—a contempt calculated

School and almshouse built by Leo XIII at Carpineto.

to convince us that philosophy can be learnt without books,
and that, to the untutored mind, life is the best school of
wisdom. "We were up with the dawn," says Salvagni, "and
clambered up to beat all the Foresta, Casino, and Casettone
coverts. Ser Nino would even venture on the Alpine slopes
of Melaina and Fageta, not to mention Semprevisa and

Capreo. How many times have we not seen the last rays of
the sun gild our footsteps on these heights, whilst the village
beneath gradually faded away in the blue smoke from the
cottage chimneys and the advancing shadows of the sur-
rounding mountains! Now-a-days Ser Nino—or Leo XIII,
as we pompously call him—is the greatest man in the world,
but the dome of St. Peter's is quite big enough to over-
shadow his prison of a palace, and long before nightfall too!
I pity him indeed!"

"Do you know how long it is since the Pope visited his
birthplace?"

"We have not seen Ser Nino since he came here on
September 30, 1857, and left us on November 2 of the same
year.

"When I went to meet him at Montelanico, with all the
sportsmen of the district, I fired what was my last salute in
his honour on the way. I was called up to load his gun, and
he fired at a quail, but missed it altogether. That was his
last shot. His gun is still at Carpineto. When we are asked
to pray for him in church, I do it readily when I think what
an unhappy Pope he must be, but I can't forgive him for not
being the jovial sportsman he was."

"One day," continued the loquacious veteran, "when
neither Ser Nino nor I had a hair on our chins, we were out
snaring larks with a net. While he was stretching one of
the cords he leant too far over the edge of the big ditch you
see yonder, and rolled right down to the bottom. I laugh
now when I think of him tumbling down through the rose-
mary and long grass growing on the side of the ditch. He

was not hurt, and got out of the ditch easily enough with the help of a stick I held out to him. He was rather angry, and when he jumped on to the road safe and sound and saw our nets all torn, he exclaimed, 'When I am Pope I will have a bridge built here.' Pope he is, right enough, but the bridge isn't built yet. It doesn't do to commit yourself, you see; you may not be able to keep your word." Evidently a philosopher, old Salvagni.

After the vacation in October 1829, Joseph resumed his studies at the Roman College with greater ardour than ever. From this time onward his letters give evidence of a steadily intensifying determination to spare no effort to reach a position which should be an honour to his family and to himself.

"Yesterday we went to see Mgr. Nicolai, who expressed a great liking for us, and has promised not to forget us," he wrote to his father on the 13th December, 1829. "He thinks, however, I ought to study theology for another two years. He undertakes to do all that is needful at the expiration of that time. He added that he would at once begin to see about what would have to be done for my admission to the Academy of the Nobility at the end of these two or three years. I begged him to do all he could for me, to bear me in mind, and not to think that expense would stand in the way when the honour of the family and the advancement of one of its members are concerned."

In August 1830 Joachim was called upon to publicly maintain a thesis at the Roman College. The preparation of this thesis took up several weeks of his time and caused him considerable anxiety. The excessive timidity from which he could never entirely free himself caused him repeated fits of nervousness. He would not have experienced such torments had not his native pride and his passionate desire to do honour to the name of Pecci rendered the apprehension of even the slightest approach to failure unendurable to him. His fears were entirely unfounded. The proceedings, which were attended by Cardinals Nicolai, Castracane, Sinibaldi, Altieri, Della Genga, and Massimo, all the leading lights, in fact, among the professed Jesuits, ended in nothing less than a triumph for the young theologian, if we may judge by the following note against the name of Joachim Pecci in the records of the Roman College:—

"*Inter theologiæ academicos, Vincentius Peccius strenue certavit de indulgentiis in aulá maximá, coram doctoribus collegii, aliisque viris doctriná spectatissimis. Quum vero in hac publicá excercitatione, academico more paratá, industrius adolescens non parvam ingenii vim et diligentiam impenderit, placuit ejus nomen, honoris causá, hic recensere.*" [1]

He bore this triumph modestly, and attributed it to his professor of theology, Father Perrone, as the two stanzas which he read to his illustrious audience after the discussion testify :—

[1] In the theological schools Vincent Pecci hath strenuously disputed, concerning indulgences, in the great hall, in presence of the doctors of the college, and of other men well proved in doctrine. And whereas, in this public exercise, held in accordance with academic customs, this industrious young man showed no little force and diligence of character, it hath seemed good to here record his name as an honorary distinction.

" Si bene quid dixi, cui gratia?   Docte magister,
   Plena est præceptis gratia habenda tuis.
Si male quid dixi, non jam culpanda voluntas ;
   Arguite ad tardum verius ingenium."[1]

Joachim even carried his modesty to the extent of
allowing more than a fortnight to elapse before sending his
family an account of this memorable day.   Finally he
announced his victory to his brother in the following terms :—

" I am not in a position to say whether everything went
well or the reverse, because no one, as the saying is, can be
a judge in his own case.   I have heard, however, that my
superiors were satisfied, and they told me the affair passed
off better than was expected."

Perhaps he was not at heart as satisfied as his superiors.
It is the privilege of exceptionally gifted natures to require
more of themselves than of others, and to judge their own
achievements with a severity bordering on injustice.   Is not
the man of genius powerless to produce anything entirely on
a par with his faculties, and has not God made this
impotence a ransom for glory ?   All men of high intelligence,
or merely of cultivated mind, feel this impotence and suffer
from it more or less.   The foolish, on the other hand, take
an innocent delight in the emptiness of their thoughts, their
words, and their acts.   This is a merciful dispensation for
which Providence should be thanked on their behalf.

Pius VIII died in December of the same year (1830),

[1] If I have well spoken, whose is the honour ?   Learned master, to
thy instruction must I render full acknowledgment.

If I have ill spoken, the fault lies not in my will but rather in the
poverty of my understanding.

after a reign of twenty-two months.   Cardinal Cappellari was
elected to succeed him on the 2nd of February, 1831, and
assumed the title of Gregory XVI.   The Conclave which
resulted in this election presented but few features of interest.
Joachim consequently gives few details of it, but he does not

John Pecci, brother of Leo XIII.

omit to show up in bold relief the intrigues carried on by
certain cardinals with the object of defeating Cappellari.
After a running commentary on these intrigues during the
Conclave he sums up the final discomfiture of the instigators
as follows:—

" ' *Annuntio vobis gaudium magnum : habemus pontificem Rmum DD. card. Maurum Cappellari, qui sibi nomen imposuit Gregorium XVI.'* (I bring you tidings of great joy : our new Pope is the Most Reverend Maurus Cappellari, who has

S. S. Leo XIII in 1843, Archbishop of Damascus and
Apostolic Nuncio in Belgium.

taken the name of Gregory XVI.) Cardinal Albani made this announcement yesterday, in the loggia of the Quirinal. He was somewhat nervous, and tried to appear indifferent."

Five weeks later he wrote :—" What a pleasure it is to me

to learn that our good Pontiff Gregory XVI is venerated and
loved by the faithful in our part of the world! His great
qualities are, in truth, such as to fit him for the sublime
dignity to which he has been raised. Come Albani, come
Pacca, or any other Cardinal after them, all must hide their
diminished heads before this resplendent luminary."

This enthusiasm, however, narrowly escaped being nipped
in the bud. The revolution broke out at Bologna on the
10th February, and all the Roman provinces were soon in
open revolt. Rome itself was threatened, and there was
some reason to fear that the "resplendent luminary" hailed
at its rising by Joachim Pecci might be completely obscured
and hidden by the storm-cloud. The danger, however, was
averted by the Austrian occupation of the Papal States. As
is well known, this occupation gave rise to an exchange of
diplomatic notes between the Holy See and France, whose
Ambassador at Rome was then the Comte de St. Aulaire.
Cardinal Bernetti was entrusted with the task of replying to
the remonstrances of the French Government, and the skill
displayed in this delicate affair by the Secretary of State
delighted the awakening diplomatic faculties of the young
student Joachim Pecci. He kept himself posted in the progress of the negotiations, and watched them with the keenest
interest. He hailed the entry of the Teutons into Bologna with
joy. He was greatly pleased when the French Government
at length showed itself favourable to the Papacy, and he
attributed this change quite as much to Cardinal Bernetti's
diplomacy as to the justice of his cause. In his letters
Joachim discusses the probable results of intervention by

Russia, Prussia, and England, and gives a well-reasoned opinion on the progress of the events which were rapidly assuming the proportions of a genuine danger to the independence of the Papacy. All his letters at this period display extraordinary sagacity. His accounts of the election of Pius VIII and Gregory XVI were characterized, as we have seen, by qualities which the most experienced "special" might envy. Now we find him writing like the most discreet of diplomatists. This implies intensely hard work on the part of this young man of twenty-one, intuitive knowledge being a myth, in diplomacy as well as in philosophy. His unremitting labour, or over-work as it would be called now-a-days, necessarily injured his health, which was never particularly robust. The month of June, 1831, brought illness to Joachim Pecci. His internal organization revolted against the strain imposed on it by prolonged vigil and study. In spite of Bossuet's assertion that a master intellect can always hold the mastery over the body it animates, Joachim Pecci's mind was forced to give way to his rebellious body. " These attacks are painful and disquieting, especially as they interfere with my studies, which are my sole concern," he writes to his brother John Baptist, July 8, 1831. It would be a mistake to suppose that he gave in altogether. His illness forced him to rest, but not to surrender. He fought hard against the malady that endeavoured in vain to overthrow him ; and he was even able to celebrate the conflict, and defy death in a fine set of verses. It is the poet's privilege to forget his ills in song. The Muse never fails to console those who invoke her.

His native air restored Joachim's health. On his return

to the Eternal City a letter from his father informed him that
the Pecci family was at last "admitted to the Anagni
nobility." There was now no obstacle to his entering the
College of the Nobility, especially as (he states in a letter to
his father) " the board-fee is only nineteen crowns up to
August 15, and another nineteen up to November 15." He
entered the institution on the 15th November, 1832. He
had already been two years an assistant master at the
Germanic College for philosophy students, and President of
the Theological Academy of the Roman College. Four
months previously the Abbé Laureani, the Arcadian
Chancellor, had handed him the diploma entitling him to join
the celebrated Academy. The rule is for every new
Arcadian, as for every new Pope, to adopt a fresh name.
The future Leo XIII chose to be called Neander Eracleus.

CHAPTER IV

THE PRELACY

THREE days before his admission to the Academy, Joachim Pecci called on Cardinal Sala, his protector and the best friend of his family. Joachim was still undecided as to the vocation he should adopt.

"Well, young man," said the Cardinal, "are you ready to take orders?"

"Oh, wait a moment, your Eminence," was the reply.

"My young friend," rejoined the Cardinal, "if all the Roman aristocracy were as undecided as you, the Holy Father might as well shut up his College of the Nobility."

Joachim Pecci's irresolution arose from a mixture of prudence and energy. If his habit was to hesitate for a considerable time before coming to any important determination, it was because he wished to make sure of his ability to prosecute his design to the very end. Never to advance without the certainty of never being obliged to recede is not a characteristic of indecision but of wisdom. Joachim was

45

received with marked favour by Mgr. Sinibaldi, the head of the Academy, which, as its name implies, was open only to ecclesiastics of noble birth intended for the Romish priesthood or diplomacy. In spite of his bad health, he soon took the first place by dint of hard work. One of his occasional competitors was Duke Diario Sforza, afterwards Archbishop of Naples and Cardinal. He had barely attended the lectures on canon law and common law a year when he was selected to maintain a public argument in the presence of the Sovereign Pontiff. In order to devote himself entirely to the preparation of a thesis likely to have such an important influence on his future, he spent his holidays with his brother John Baptist at Maenza. "At Carpineto," he wrote to his brother, "there are too many festivities and amusements. Study requires solitude, which, to my mind, ought to be unbroken and even melancholy." He found what he required at Maenza, but his solitude was more melancholy than he could have wished. He had hardly reached his brother's house when he was attacked by a severe throat complaint, and was obliged to take a prolonged rest. During his vacation his sufferings left him little opportunity for work, and when he returned to Rome, eager to make up for lost time, he studied so hard as to again, and more seriously, endanger his health. His medical attendant, Dr. Cavallini, was obliged to forbid work altogether, and the great argument *coram sanctissimo*, which he hoped would open up a "most brilliant career" to him, was postponed. As the argument would have cost him "at least 700 crowns," its postponement was a great saving, and, poor as he was, this could not fail to be a consideration. The following passage in one of his letters, written about this period to John Baptist, is significant :—

"This morning I received four more numbers of Valadier, for which I have paid out eighteen *paoli* on your account. This makes six crowns in all. You know my poverty, and the feeling of prudence which forbids my allowing you to run up too large a debt. This is all the more reason why you should send me the amount on the first opportunity."

Joachim Pecci delivered his first public dissertation at the Academy of the Nobility on the 6th May, 1835. The Pope did not attend, but the presence of five cardinals—Macchi, Sala, Castracane, Polidori, and Mattei—and numerous prelates increased the *éclat* of the occasion. Not long afterwards the future Pope took part in a special competitive debate on public ecclesiastical law, the question for treatment being "Direct appeal to the person of the Sovereign Pontiff." For this he obtained a prize of thirty sequins. His most complete and fruitful triumph, however, was in September 1835, when he delivered a disquisition dedicated to Cardinal Sala. That prelate, Joachim writes, attended "in full state and in purple." This time Joseph does himself the justice of admitting that the affair was successful in every respect, and adds :—"I have acquired a powerful protector in Cardinal Sala, who is a prelate of the highest standing." Sala was the former counsellor of Cardinal Caprera, and played an active part in the negotiations which paved the way for the Concordat. The most eminent among the princes of the Church were glad to have recourse to his advice, and the Pope valued him highly. His protection could not but be, and in fact was, of great importance to Joachim. The latter had taken the lesser orders in 1834, but was not to have applied for admission to the sub-diaconate until the end of the year 1837. In the course of that year, however,

Entrance to the Vatican—the Swiss Guards' Gate.

he was successively appointed one of his Holiness'˙ prelates, referee of the Papal signature, and ponent of the Buongoverno congregation, where-in all the adminis-trative business of the Papal States was transacted. Mgr. Pecci was the junior prelate when he was given this post, in succession to Mgr. Amici. Cardinal Sala's influence could not have been un-connected with so speedy a promotion.

The rapidity of Mgr. Pecci's advancement in the diplo-matic career affords a striking contrast to the slowness of his preferment in holy orders. As we know, he respectfully but firmly declined to accede to the wishes of his mother and Monsignor the delegate in regard to the tonsure, and

Leo XIII when Nuncio at Brussels, with his relatives, in 1807.

we have read of his hesitation on the eve of taking the lesser orders. "Wait a moment," he said to Cardinal Sala. This "moment" lasted two years, and three more elapsed before he appears to have thought of definitely entering the service of the Church by taking the first of the full orders. He was, as we have already stated, a prelate, referee of the Papal signature and ponent, all before he became a sub-deacon. At this period it was in the ordinary course for a man to make his way in the Papal civil service or diplomacy without taking rank in the priesthood. It is none the less curious that at the age of twenty-seven the future Leo XIII was apparently given up to ambition in which the next world had no visible influence, and was not an aspirant to the honour of standing before the altar. His mental attitude is shown clearly enough in a letter dated the 3rd July, 1837, to his brother Charles at Carpineto. The letter is worth reading from beginning to end. Every word helps to throw light on the writer's mind :—

"Your letter of the 1st inst. gave me the utmost pleasure, and your prognostications of my advancement were a great comfort to me. With all the sincerity I am accustomed to use in my affairs, and especially in regard to my relatives, I can assure you that since the day on which, to meet my father's wishes, I entered upon my present career, I have had but one object : to devote all my energies to following a praiseworthy line of conduct with a view to rising in the Pontifical service, so that whatever honour and credit I may obtain may redound to the reputation of our family, which has, thank God, hitherto not been without such honour. In arriving at this end I believe I shall amply fulfil my father's expectations, which it will be my care never to disappoint as long as I live. Young as I am, I cannot fail to do credit to my family if my conduct is irreproachable and if I am not without protectors, these two conditions being indis-

pensable in Rome, as you know, to safe and rapid advancement.
Although I have been a prelate only five months, I have already made
the first step upward. You will no doubt be very glad to hear that
Cardinal Sala has definitely taken me under his protection, and that I
have some credit, assuredly undeserved, with the two Secretaries of
State. The Sovereign Pontiff himself regards me with favour. I had a
further proof of this yesterday during an audience in which his Holiness,
whom I begged to accept my grateful thanks, received me with special
kindness and condescension."

The foregoing letter might very well find a place in the
records of a general inquiry into the youthful ideals of our
most illustrious living men.   It might, however, give the
reader a false idea of the writer's character, of which it dis-
closes only one side.   It shows us merely a young man justifi-
ably anxious to uphold the worldly honour of his name. Other
documents from the same source set forth the tender and
unfailing piety of Father Ubaldini's *angioletto*. In September
Mgr. Pecci, having experienced some symptoms of the cholera
then ravaging Rome, wrote his will. It was such as might
have been expected from a truly and deeply religious man.

"In the name of God, Amen.
"I commend my soul to God and the most holy Mary. May
the Divine Majesty and the blessed Virgin have mercy on me, a
sinner !
"I bequeath all my worldly possessions in equal shares to my very
dear brothers Charles and John Baptist, on condition that they cause
fifty masses for the repose of my soul to be said every year for five
years.   At the end of that period they may consider themselves as
relieved of this obligation, but I appeal to their charity to increase the
number of intercessions for my soul. I further enjoin on my heirs
above-named to make one distribution of twenty crowns among the
poor of Carpineto, my native place.
"As a humble token of respect and affection, I bequeath to my uncle

Antony the porcelain service presented to me by his Eminence Cardinal Sala.

"These are the last wishes of me, Joachim Vincent Pecci, written with my own hand this 14th of September, 1837, in the third hour of the night."

It will be observed that this will contains no mention of Count Pecci. The explanation is simple. Mgr. Pecci's father had died during the previous year at Carpineto. Happily it did not become necessary to carry out the prelate's "last wishes." Vigorous medical treatment sufficed to eradicate the disease, and Mgr. Pecci was enabled to spend the greater part of his time at the bedside of the sick, tending them with all the devotion of a sister of charity, and displaying a zeal and self-sacrifice worthy of his old masters the Jesuits. "Not one of the Fathers," he exultantly writes, "has been attacked, and yet they are to be seen day and night among the plague-stricken, in every quarter and every parish of the city." Like the Jesuits, he was ready to lay down his life. "If I am to be numbered amongst the victims, I bow my head in submission to the will of the Most High, to whom I have already devoted my life in expiation of my faults. Whatever may happen, my mind is perfectly tranquil."

The Most High did not accept the offered sacrifice of Mgr. Pecci's life. He was reserved for other purposes. What was perhaps the reward of his heroism came in the shape of a vocation for the priesthood. He was admitted a sub-deacon on the 17th December, 1837, by Mgr. Sinibaldi, at the Ecclesiastical Academy. Seven days later Mgr. Sinibaldi also conferred the diaconate upon him, and on the

31st December Cardinal Odescalchi consecrated him priest for ever: *Tu es sacerdos in æternum.*

The Pontifical throne.

The period of preparation for taking the full órders of the priesthood was spent by Mgr. Pecci in silence and meditation with the Jesuit Fathers of St. Andrew. His hesitation was at an end, but he none the less awaited the honour and burden of the priesthood "with fear and trembling," to use the Scriptural expression. "This im-

Swiss Guards preceding the Pontifical procession.

portant step," he wrote in all humility to Cardinal Sala, "fills me with dread, when I consider the height and sublimity of the sacred office and my extreme unworthiness. Do not forget me, your Eminence; pray earnestly and desire

the prayers of others for me. I sincerely assure you that
I wish to be a *true priest*, to serve God and show true zeal
for His glory." So strong indeed was this desire, that he
was on the point of joining the illustrious Society of Jesus,
whose members have from the very beginning constituted
the moral and intellectual *élite* of the Roman Catholic
clergy.

Much to his joy, his first mass was celebrated, at the
St. Andrew's Institute for Novices, in the little chapel dedicated to St. Stanislas Kostka, the favourite saint of his
youth. On the following day he wrote thus to Cardinal
Sala :—

"Your Eminence says in your last note, 'I admire your fervour,
but you must not abandon the career you have begun. It may enable
you to render important services to the Church and the Holy See.' I
must reveal to your Eminence a secret which I have hitherto kept
locked in my own breast. For some time past I have felt strongly
inclined to renounce worldly pursuits and to devote myself entirely to
the inner, spiritual life. I am, in fact, convinced that the world cannot
give the heart full contentment and quietude. So great is my esteem
and admiration for the Jesuit Fathers, from whom I have imbibed all
I know, that I should have become a Jesuit had I been able to recognize
within myself something more than an inclination—the special vocation
which should be felt for the ministry."

It is to be supposed that if Cardinal Sala had thought fit
to guide Mgr. Pecci towards a purely ecclesiastical career, he
would have offered few objections to pursuing the same path
as his brother Joseph, who had just taken part for the
first time in the celebration of mass. The eminent prelate's
long experience, however, had made him an excellent judge
of character, and, as we have seen, he was chiefly inclined to

consider the "important services" Mgr. Pecci seemed likely
to render, in either the civil or diplomatic service, "to the
Church and the Holy See." When Gregory XVI was
lamenting one day over the state of insubordination prevailing in the province of Benevento, the Cardinal ventured to
say—

"You need a man of energy."

"That is true," said the Pope, "and I am afraid our
delegate does not answer to that description. It would perhaps be wise to replace him, but by whom?"

"I believe Mgr. Pecci would succeed perfectly, in spite of
his youth," replied the Cardinal. "I have had several opportunities of seeing what he can do, and I am convinced that
your Holiness could not make a better choice."

Cardinal Lambruschini, who was present, expressed a
similar opinion. On the same day, the 2nd February, 1838,
Mgr. Pecci was despatched as Papal delegate to the province
of Benevento.

CHAPTER V

FROM BENEVENTO TO PERUGIA

Delegate to Benevento—A province overrun with brigands—A
"Resurrection"—Triumph—Delegate to Perugia—Reception of Gregory
XVI—Opening of the Via Gregoriana.

THE province of Benevento was part of the old kingdom
of Naples, and is not far from the capital. The new delegate
had been ordered to take immediate possession of the post to
which he had been appointed by the confidence of Gregory
XVI. He consequently set out without delay, attended only
by five Carpineto peasants, who, being all descended from the
same family, were all called Capucci (in English, cauliflowers).
Unfortunately they possessed the same unskilfulness as well
as the same name, and their not very zealous attempts to
prepare Mgr. Pecci's simple meals met with so little success
that their master humorously observed, " E con tanti
Capucci non posso fare una menestra." (With all these
cauliflowers I cannot make a single soup.)

Mgr. Pecci kept his Carpinetans, but the brigandage prevailing all over his new province left him neither time nor
inclination for the cultivation of puns. The government of
the Ecclesiastical States was so gentle, so paternal, and at the

same time so feeble, that criminals of all kinds were in the habit of taking refuge from the Naples police in the province of Benevento, where they were almost certain of being able to continue their exploits with impunity. This state of things excited general indignation. The public protested strongly, and the Neapolitans also complained bitterly of the Pontifical Government's ill-advised tolerance. The new delegate was consequently hailed with an enthusiasm which showed plainly enough what was expected of him. "All the leading men of the province," he writes to his brother Charles, "came to meet me, and I entered the town with more than fifty carriages in my train." He had hardly arrived before he was seized with illness. As soon as the serious nature of the case became known, the inhabitants marched in a body to the sanctuary of Our Lady of Pardon and implored the Madonna to restore Mgr. Pecci's valuable health. The Madonna heard their prayer. Mgr. Pecci, whom the doctors declared to be at death's door and beyond all possibility of recovery, was miraculously restored to the strength required for his mission. In the words of his brother John Baptist, who nursed him six weeks with never-failing devotion, he was "a dead man brought back to life."

The necessity for prompt and vigorous action against the brigands was shown clearly enough by their increased audacity. They were convinced that the new delegate would have enough to do to re-establish his health. Mgr. Pecci began by satisfying himself that the Pontifical troops could be relied upon. He then drew up his plans of campaign with the utmost secrecy. He obtained the fullest information

on the districts in which brigandage chiefly flourished, and
despatched columns of troops, led by reliable and experienced
guides. The result soon surpassed all expectations. Most of
the robber chiefs were arrested and their gangs dispersed.
With a view to restoring confidence among the people,
Mgr. Pecci had the dreaded chiefs loaded with chains and
marched through the streets of the city. He also took
care that all the sentences passed by the courts were
carried out to the letter. And brigandage died out, for want
of brigands.

Having thus discharged the first duty devolving on
justice, the delegate turned his attention to the powerful
nobles who carried on the brigand business on a larger scale,
openly holding person and property for ransom, smuggling
incessantly, and often appearing at the head of their armed
forces on the main roads. Their raiding expeditions completed, they retired into their fortified castles, where the
revenue officers were powerless to reach them. With the
approval of Ferdinand II, King of Naples, Mgr. Pecci reorganized the Customs service, and placed it under the
direction of Sterpi, one of the most valuable officials in the
Papal service. A fierce struggle between the Customs officers
and the smugglers began, and soon ended in the complete
defeat of the latter, in spite of the insolent attempts of some
of the nobility to intimidate the delegate. One of them
having complained against the revenue officers for making a
search on his premises, Mgr. Pecci quietly pointed out that
the laws were made for rich and poor alike, and that every
one must submit to them.

"Very good," exclaimed the Marquis; "I shall go to Rome at once, and I shall not return until I have obtained the recall of the Benevento delegate."

"The Benevento delegate does not in the least desire to prevent your going," quietly replied Mgr. Pecci. "He merely wishes to remind you that you cannot reach the Vatican without going through the Castle of St. Angelo."

The threat contained in these words was not lost on the titled adventurer. The prospect of an enforced stay in the celebrated fortress had no charms for him. Instead of proceeding to the Eternal City, he returned post-haste to his château and prepared to defend it. The Pontifical troops made their appearance a few days afterwards, and captured the place after a regular siege.

In this way the province of Benevento, thanks to the delegate's energy, was cleared in a few months of the bandits of all kinds who had infested it for years. Mgr. Pecci did not stop here. He opened new roads for trade, obtained reductions in the most burdensome of the taxes, and carried out quite a series of public reforms, in spite of the opposition of certain interested parties. He was soon able to write to his brother Charles :—"The affairs of the province are now in order, and the opinion of the majority, of the people I mean, is in my favour. Duty is my guide, and I make it my rule never to have my hands tied by personal considerations. These tactics do not greatly please the upper classes, but they have earned me the reputation of a friend of justice, and they satisfy the public and my own conscience." They evidently satisfied the Pontifical Government as well. The

Pope warmly praised the delegate for "the reforms he had
carried out, and the good results he had obtained." King
Ferdinand invited Mgr. Pecci to visit his Court and receive
public proof of the royal esteem.

Mgr. Pecci had spent three years in Benevento. When
his work in that province was accomplished, he was

The Pope's bearers.

appointed delegate to Spoleto, but Gregory XVI soon
realized that it was time to open a wider sphere to the
young prelate's activity. Mgr. Pecci had barely begun to
prepare for his departure from Benevento, when he received
an official notification of his appointment as delegate to
Perugia.

General view of the Vatican gardens.

This ancient city, with its feudal towers and hundred churches, stands on a mountain overlooking the green plains of Umbria. In Mgr. Pecci's time the city was by no means easy of access. It seemed as if the inhabitants were content to enjoy the splendid view before them, without wishing to mingle with their fellow-creatures below. Mgr. Pecci had only just reached Perugia when Gregory XVI announced his intention of visiting the city. The delegate had only twenty days to organize a reception for the Pope on a scale appropriate to royalty. The time, however, was so well utilized that a magnificent new artery was completed. It was opened by the Sovereign Pontiff on the 25th September, 1841, amid the acclamations of a populace as yet uncorrupted by the revolutionary virus, in spite of the incessant efforts of the secret societies. The new road was christened the "Via Gregoriana." The Pope, whose name had been given to it, expressed his satisfaction by saying that during his journey through the provinces he had been received in some places like a monk, in others like a cardinal, and at Perugia and Ancona like a sovereign. Before his departure, the Pope gave a hint of the good fortune in store for his delegate by saying, "When I return to Rome, Monsignor, I will remember you." The Pope kept his word. At the commencement of the year 1843 Mgr. Pecci was appointed Nuncio at Brussels in the place of Mgr. Fornari, who was transferred to Paris. During his eighteen months' stay at Perugia, Mgr. Pecci had reorganized all the provincial government departments, and especially those connected with public instruction and the administration of justice. In his desire to

F

improve the condition of the working classes, he even founded a savings bank. His record was one of good work executed with a promptitude remarkable in a young man who had been formerly reproached by Cardinal Sala for "indecision."

CHAPTER VI

NUNCIO AT BRUSSELS

THOUGH less important than any of the four great nunci-atures—Paris, Vienna, Madrid, and Munich—the post at Brussels is assuredly one of the most agreeable. " What a delightful country you have ! " observed Mgr. Fornari to a Belgian statesman. " I have spent five years in it, and I feel as if I had been five years in Paradise." This paradise was none the less, for a nuncio at the commencement of his dip-lomatic career, the most interesting observatory that he could have desired, especially at this period, when Belgium, as has been very justly said, " was a condensed edition of the struggles, the successes, the aspirations and the mistakes of modern social organizations." The situation, moreover, could not but be an especially delicate one for Mgr. Pecci, in view of the events which had preceded his appointment. The sudden recall of Mgr. Fornari, who was on much better terms with the Government than with the Belgian bishops, was far from pleasing to the King. Mgr. Garibaldi, inter-nuncio at the French Court, had been selected by the Pope to succeed Mgr. Fornari, but the King had not approved the nomination. These circumstances could not but bring about a coolness in the future intercourse between the two Powers, and it appeared unlikely that Mgr. Pecci would secure the good graces of both ·the Government and the Episcopate, especially as the conflict between the episcopal body and the Minister of the Interior, M. Nothomb, over the Elementary Education Act, had just reached its most acute stage.

In view of these facts, the new Nuncio probably experienced more uneasiness than delight when he heard from the Pope's own mouth, at Rome, of the honour intended for him, and the burden about to fall on his shoulders. "This duty," he wrote to Cardinal Bussi, Archbishop of Benevento, "causes me great anxiety. I do not undertake it through presumption, but in filial obedience to the sovereign Pastor and in resignation to the mysterious purposes of Heaven." To Mgr. di Andrea, Nuncio to Switzerland, he wrote :—" I am now your comrade in the glorious arena of religion, but what hope of victory have I ? On what source of strength can I base that hope ? I prefer to dismiss these disturbing thoughts, and place my whole trust in One who has begun the task and is able to accomplish it. I have no hope but in Him." He also confided his fears to a Passionist, the head of the order of Jesus Crucified, who replied :—" Courage. Trust in God and not in yourself. You are destined to great things."

Mistrust of self would hardly have been inspired in the new Nuncio had he read the rhymed effusion perpetrated about this time in his honour by one of his compatriots, the Abbé Gessi. " As the sun outshines the bright stars, so is Joachim pre-eminent in glory, honour, and resplendent virtues. Now a wearer of the cross and the violet robe, he shall one day put on the purple and the bissus, and shall rise still higher. Like Jove's eagle, he shall perch upon the rocky summit. *It is written in the Eternal Book of Fate, that he shall be crowned with the tiara and hold the sceptre. I see him seated on a lofty throne, the cross on his breast and the tiara on his brow. Italy, the Low Countries, France, England, the shore of Africa itself shall see and admire his virtues. Some day he shall be adored on earth, his glory shall be seated on the throne, and the omnipotent God who rules over all shall make him the Shepherd of Christ's flock."*

La Fontaine has told us that fools sometimes sell wisdom. The saying certainly applies to the Carpineto "poet," whose prophecies, absurdly grandiloquent and improbable as they appeared, have nevertheless been fulfilled to the letter.

Mgr. Fornari, who was less lyrical than the Abbé Gessi, and an incontestably better judge, expressed the following opinion of his successor in a letter to M. Noyer, the Belgian *chargé d'affaires* in Rome :—" There can be no doubt that Mgr. Pecci is a prelate of great piety, talent, and acquirements. He is perhaps somewhat timid, or rather his extreme modesty resembles timidity, but this is amply made up for by his power of reflection and his prudence, which will always secure him against a false step. He is so conscientious and upright that he will leave no stone unturned to carry out all his duties, and do useful service to the good cause."

It being customary for nuncios to be also bishops, Mgr. Pecci was raised to the episcopate immediately after his appointment to Brussels. Gregory XVI proclaimed him Archbishop of Damietta on the 27th January, and on the 28th Cardinal Lambruschini, the Secretary of State, consecrated him in the basilica of St. Lawrence *in Panisperna*,

View of the Vatican gardens from the entrance.

in the presence of Count d'Oultremont and the staff of the Belgian Legation. After the ceremony Cardinal Lambruschini, who knew the deep piety of Mgr. Pecci, said of him :— " He is an angel. He is my favourite son."

The new Nuncio embarked at Civita Vecchia on the 19th March, on board the French ship *Sesostris*. He reached Belgium on the 7th April, sickness having detained him at

Nîmes about ten days, which he managed to utilize by taking lessons in French. At the time of his departure from the capital of Christianity, the Archbishop of Damietta had an only slight acquaintance with the language of diplomacy, but when he arrived at Brussels he was able to express himself in French with correctness and even elegance. Fifty-four years

The Vatican gardens—Vinery of Leo XIII.

later the recollection of this feat provided him with an argument against the Cardinals who tried to persuade him not to send the Bishop of Viterbo to Paris as Nuncio, for what they considered the all-sufficient reason that Mgr. Clari did not know French well enough. "If he does not know French," replied Leo XIII, "let him learn it, as I did when Gregory XVI made me Nuncio to Belgium half-a-century ago."

Mgr. Pecci's knowledge of French was within an ace of becoming superfluous even before he had an opportunity of using it. On the road to Brussels his carriage-horses took fright, and bolted while crossing the Vilvoorde canal, but a catastrophe was averted by the heroism of a priest of a neighbouring parish, who saved the young prelate's life at the risk of his own. Mgr. Pecci, who was an excellent walker, finished the journey on foot.

Reference has already been made to the conflict created by the Education Act of 1842, between the Belgian episcopate and the Minister of the Interior. This Act recognized the religious character of the primary schools to a certain extent; but the Government, preferring complete neutrality, applied the law in a very half-hearted way. In a certain letter dated the 26th January, 1843, the Belgian bishops had protested against the equivocal attitude of the authorities. Immediately upon his arrival at Brussels, Mgr. Pecci was urgently requested to use his influence to silence the bishops. He preferred to incur the Minister's displeasure, and directed his action entirely towards the support of the bishops' just claims. It was an openly uncompromising policy, sufficiently justified by the attack on the imprescriptible rights of the Church in educational matters. Mgr. Pecci soon found it necessary to accentuate his resistance. The Government claimed to be allowed to appoint all the members of the examining boards, two-thirds of whom were, *de jure*, selected by the Chambers. The Belgian Catholics unanimously protested through their bishops, and the young Nuncio's diplomacy gave them such vigorous and useful support, that

M. Nothomb's Bill was rejected by a large majority. The Minister bore a grudge against the representative of the Holy See for a long time after this event, if we may judge by a letter to M. d'Hoffschmidt, dated the 14th November, 1847, more than two years after M. Nothomb had left office :—"The departure of Mgr. Fornari was a great misfortune, and his successor has made me regret the non-arrival of Mgr. Garibaldi." The Nuncio's credit at Court, however, was by no means diminished. "Really, Monsignor," King Leopold I said to him one day, "you are as good a politician as you are a prelate." The King, moreover, did not confine himself to empty compliments. He sought opportunities to discuss the religious interests of the kingdom with Mgr. Pecci, listened to him with pleasure, gave way to his arguments without too much resistance, and sometimes granted his requests. As an instance, the King carried his condescension so far as to be present, with the Queen, at the ceremony of crowning the figure of Notre Dame de la Chapelle on the 25th May, 1843, and to accompany her Majesty soon afterwards on her visit to the school in connection with the Sacred Heart of Jette. As King Leopold belonged to the Protestant religion, the influence acquired by Mgr. Pecci over his Majesty was all the more remarkable. As for Queen Marie Louise, who was a fervent Catholic, she admired the Prelate's virtues still more than his diplomatic skill. She freely consulted him, not on affairs of State but on the princes' education, and adopted his advice. Mgr. Pecci always looked back with something more than pleasure to the many hours he spent with the King and Queen as their guest. When Cardinal at Perugia, he remarked one day to a Belgian bishop, "I well knew your present King's father and pious mother. I was often admitted to the friendly intimacy of the royal family, and I have held the little Leopold, Duke of Brabant, in my arms. I remember that good Christian, Queen Marie Louise, asking me to give my benediction to her eldest son, then eight or nine years old, so that he might become a good king."

The Belgians themselves made quite as favourable an impression as their sovereigns on Mgr. Pecci. "I cannot," he writes, "but praise the kindliness and strong religious feeling of this people." Elsewhere he speaks of the "good and hospitable nature" of King Leopold's subjects, and refers with admiration to the state of development attained by the national industries. Italy being at that time without railways, he sends his friends a full account of the opening of the railway between Brussels and Namur, at which he was present with all the diplomatic body. "Nothing is more agreeable than riding like this at more than twenty miles an hour. The most delightful views, villas, country houses, and villages, sped past on our right and left like a dream or an optical illusion." The Nuncio's attention was not, of course, entirely absorbed by matters of industrial progress. He was greatly interested in everything relating to education. We have already mentioned the part he took in the discussion excited by the application of the Education Act. He intervened with equal success in the conflict to which this Act gave rise between the University of Louvain and the Jesuit College at Namur. The heads of the College

attempted to introduce certain reforms which could not fail
to excite the suspicions of the University authorities. A
fairly large number of bishops sided with the College, and
others with the University. The Nuncio suggested to the
Episcopate that the matter should be referred to the Holy
See, and he was skilful enough to obtain a Papal decision
calculated to satisfy both parties. At the same time he
used all his influence towards the foundation, at Rome, of a
Belgian ecclesiastical college, which he endowed with royal
liberality immediately after his own elevation to the sovereign
Pontificate. He also drew up regulations defining the
relations between the religious orders and the bishops. The
regular clergy were then under the control of a Vicar
Apostolic, who was not only aged and infirm, but very weak
in character. Mgr. Pecci asked Gregory XVI for the necessary authority to make up for the deficiencies of the Vicar
Apostolic. This authority was granted him, and he soon
succeeded in accomplishing this very delicate task, which
Mgr. Fornari, with whom he frequently corresponded, invariably represented as extremely dangerous.

The Nuncio thus triumphed on all sides, but with a
moderation and wisdom which could not fail to excite
admiration. When, after his three years' service as Nuncio,
he was summoned to the see of Perugia, he received in-
numerable proofs of respect and liking, not only in religious
but in political circles—an eloquent testimony to the good
he had accomplished, and the general regret caused by his
departure. "Thanks to your Excellency," wrote General
Goblet, ex-Minister of Foreign Affairs, "our relations were

characterized by a cordiality and good feeling which made
my task as easy as it was agreeable." Cardinal Stercks,
Archbishop of Mechlin, told him :—"The inhabitants of the
fortunate diocese of Perugia will gain a bishop distinguished
by knowledge and piety, and a model of all the virtues. I

The Pontifical guard.

greatly regret that you are obliged to leave us so soon.
Your excellent intentions, your wise views, and your zeal
for the prosperity of our religion would have been of so
much further service to us." And the Cardinal closed his
letter by assuring Mgr. Pecci of his "eternal gratitude."

Uniforms of the household troops of Leo XIII.

The King sent an equally flattering message through his secretary, M. de Bonway, and gave Mgr. Pecci the grand cordon of the Order of Leopold. The King did not stop here, but sent Gregory XVI a letter in which the old monarch's personal friendship for the Nuncio is strikingly shown. Leopold I wrote, regardless of official ceremony, and evidently less regretting the diplomatist than the friend he was about to lose:—"I desire to recommend Archbishop Pecci to your Holiness's kind protection. He thoroughly deserves it, for I have rarely seen a more sincere devotion to duty, more upright conduct, or more excellent intentions. His stay in this country has enabled him to do good service both to your Holiness and himself. I beg your Holiness to request him to give a full statement of his views on Belgian ecclesiastical affairs. His judgment is correct, and your Holiness can place full confidence in him."

The Archbishop's departure was thus the occasion for a general expression of esteem and regret. These sentiments were not experienced on one side only, for Mgr. Pecci had learnt to love the Belgian people. He introduced several Belgian industries into Perugia, his episcopal palace was always open to Belgian visitors, and whenever the affairs of his diocese took him to Rome, it was his custom to ask for hospitality at the Belgian Ecclesiastical College. He left many tried and proved friends among the Brussels aristocracy. Among these were the ex-President of the Senate, M. de Mérode, in whose splendid garden the Nuncio loved to read his breviary ; the Comte de Baillet, and the Baron de Man. When the latter's name was mentioned before the Pope, many years afterwards, his Holiness immediately exclaimed :—"Good de Man, I have not forgotten him ! He used to regularly divide his income of 100,000 fr. into two parts—50,000 fr. for himself and 50,000 fr. for the poor. Afterwards he discovered that 50,000 fr. was too much for him, and he reduced his own allowance to 25,000 fr." From which it would appear that the Pope has not only a good heart, but a good memory for figures.

Though Mgr. Pecci's health was indifferently suited to the comparatively cold climate of Belgium, it is easy to understand the regret he experienced in leaving a country which had been so hospitable to him. He perhaps hardly realized that this regret had some share in the weight of uneasiness inspired by the prospect of the new responsibilities awaiting him. Writing to Mgr. Spinelli, one of the *Auditores Rotæ*,[1] to whom Mgr. Pecci attributed his nomination to the see of Perugia, he says :—"Will your hopes be realized as you expect ? I must frankly confess that when I examine myself I find no cause for anything but fear and confusion. In spite of my very keen desire to do good at Perugia, I fear my feeble efforts will not suffice to make that desire fruitful."

[1] The Rota is a judicial department of the Pontificate, consisting of twelve learned dignitaries called Auditors of the Rota, selected from prelates of Italian, French, German, and Spanish nationality.—Trans.

CHAPTER VII

THIRTY-TWO YEARS A BISHOP

Visit to England and France—Death of Gregory XVI and accession of Pius IX—Letter from the new Pope to the King of the Belgians—Mgr. Pecci's entry into Perugia—The Revolution—The Perugia clergy—Urban Ratazzi on the Bishop—A seaside meeting—Pecci and Antonelli—The end of a reign.

MGR. PECCI did not return at once to Italy from Brussels. He visited Germany, Austria, and England, making the acquaintance of Cardinal Wiseman in London, and obtaining the honour of a presentation to the Queen. Wiseman supplied him with reliable information as to the state of Catholicism in England. Mgr. Pecci next went to Paris, and spent three weeks as the guest of Mgr. Fornari, who secured him a long interview with Louis Philippe. During his stay in Paris Mgr. Pecci several times celebrated mass in the church of St. Thomas Aquinas, and a few years ago he reminded the *curé* of that parish of the fact. On his return to Paris the *curé*, M. Ravailhe, conceived the idea of commemorating the event by placing a marble tablet, with an appropriate inscription, in the church, but, owing to his retirement, the plan has not yet been carried out.

From Paris Mgr. Pecci proceeded to Rome. On his arrival he found that Gregory XVI was dead, and that the members of the Sacred College were already assembled in the Conclave which was to result in the election of Pius IX. The new Bishop of Perugia had a long conversation with Cardinal Ferreti on the position of the Church. The interview between the two future Popes is a singularly interesting event, when the destiny common to both and the difference in their methods of thought are taken into account. Some time after his elevation to the Papacy as Pius IX, Cardinal Mastaï Ferreti reminded the Bishop of Perugia of this conversation. It was Pius IX who answered the letter in which King Leopold had so strongly recommended the former Nuncio at Brussels to Gregory XVI. The answer, full of promise for the subject of the correspondence, was as follows:—" Your Majesty's testimony in favour of Mgr. Pecci, Bishop of Perugia, does that prelate great honour. He will in due time reap the benefit of your Majesty's kindly recommendation, exactly as if he had not abandoned the diplomatic career." The "due time" came eight years later. Mgr. Pecci, who was proclaimed Bishop of Perugia, and created Cardinal *in petto* on the 19th January, 1846, did not receive the purple robe until the consistory of the 19th December, 1853.

We have several times had occasion to dwell upon the filial piety of Joachim Pecci. Since his parents' death, it had become a cherished custom with him to connect their memory with the principal events of his life. " Oh, if only my dear parents were still alive !" was his first exclamation on hearing of his appointment to the nunciature at Brussels ;

and now that he was about to reach another and still more
glorious period of his ecclesiastical career, he selected the 26th
July, the day of St. Anne, his mother's patron saint, for taking
possession of his see. His entry into the city in which he
had done such great things as delegate was nothing less than
a triumph. He was conducted to the cathedral in solemn
procession, the *cortège* comprising all the civil and religious
officials and the University professors in their robes. Mgr.
Pecci, wearing his mitre and full episcopal insignia, rode on a
fine horse caparisoned with white. Over his head was a
baldaquin carried by eight attendants in white cottas.[1] The
prelate was preceded by a band of children belonging to the
best families in the city, who strewed handfuls of flowers in
the new Bishop's path. It was a grand and touching
spectacle, suggestive of another occasion on which the people
cast their garments and olive-branches beneath the feet of
One far greater than the Bishop of Perugia.

Mgr. Pecci's term of office was very stormy, but fruitful—
stormy, because he was twice, in 1849 and 1860, brought
face to face with a revolution. In 1849 the Garibaldians
took possession of the city, and the Austrians, under the
command of Prince von Lichtenstein, were preparing to
attack them when Mgr. Pecci intervened, with the result that
order was restored without bloodshed. Eleven years afterwards, the 14th September, 1860, Perugia was captured by an
army of 15,000 Piedmontese under General de Sonnaz. The
enemy took possession of the seminary and the Bishop's
palace. All that Mgr. Pecci could do was to implore the

---

[1] Cotta, or cota, a short surplice.—Trans.

conqueror's clemency for the inhabitants. In spite of this
appeal an ecclesiastic named Santi, who was wrongfully
accused of firing on the Piedmontese, was shot. The Bishop
subsequently made no less than nine indignant protests
against the excesses committed by the conquerors. It was
also his painful duty to lay an interdict on several priests

The Vatican gardens—the Swiss summer-house.

who had forgotten their duty towards the Sovereign Pontiff.
These priests actually had the audacity to take legal
proceedings against the head of the diocese, and though Mgr.
Pecci was acquitted, it can easily be imagined how greatly his
feelings, both as a priest and the father of his clergy, were
wounded.

Amidst the general upheaval the Bishop of Perugia

remained more closely united than ever to the Bishop of Rome. Below is the noble letter he wrote to Pius IX after the events of the 28th January, 1860:

"MOST HOLY FATHER,

"The Cardinal Bishop of Perugia and the whole Chapter of his cathedral, deeply deploring the impious and cowardly attacks con-

The Vatican gardens—the Swiss summer-house.

stantly made on the Holy See, humbly assure you of their filial duty and submission. They keenly sympathize with the bitter sufferings that wring your Holiness' paternal heart. They weep for the blindness and malice of those ungrateful and degenerate sons who have joined with the enemies of the Church against its august head. They indignantly denounce the underhand manœuvres employed to seize upon your secular sovereignty, and the perfidious attempts to strip the Sovereign Pontiff of his dignity and independence by stirring up rebellion and schism in the very centre of Catholic unity. In common with the

whole of Christianity they protest against such dark designs, and they
pray the Prince of Shepherds, whose living oracle and august vicar
you are, that He will not permit the accomplishment of these guilty and
sacrilegious machinations, and that He will again make patent to all, in
your august person, that St. Peter's chair is the corner-stone against
which all human effort is vain. May this humble token of love, laid by
the undersigned at your feet on behalf of the entire Church in Perugia,
assuage your grief! They implore your benediction, and pray that it
may render them ever steadfast in their obedience to you as well as in
the profession and defence of Catholic unity."

Five months later (June 21), the courageous prelate ventured to appeal to the King himself against the unworthy
treatment which the Government Commissioner, believing
himself secure from punishment, did not hesitate to inflict on
members of the religious orders in the diocese. The Bishop
wrote:—"This, Sire, is how the royal decrees are set at
naught by want of fairness in their application. Many
excellent and worthy ecclesiastics must inevitably suffer from
the harsh and oppressive measures of the royal Commissioner
—measures which are not only without a parallel in other
provinces, but are moreover altogether out of harmony with
the most elementary conceptions of the social rights of religion.
The outcome of such conduct ought not to remain unknown
to your Majesty. In hereby denouncing it, I cannot but
express the painful feeling of bitterness which I, as a Bishop,
experience in witnessing the repeated insults directed against
the true interests of religion, and the wretched condition to
which the ecclesiastics now living amongst us are reduced."
Mgr. Pecci had previously protested with the utmost energy
against the introduction of secular marriages. His efforts
were not always crowned with success, but they did not

remain altogether fruitless, and his courageous attitude, if it
brought no practical result, at least had the appreciable
advantage of extorting admiration and respect from the
bitterest adversaries of the Church, as the two following
letters from Urban Ratazzi to his wife testify :—

"This Pecci is a man of undeniable merit. He is gifted with great
energy and power of management, coupled with the mildest manners
imaginable. The fact is that, in spite of his incorruptibility and loftiness of mind, and in spite of the deep-rooted respect he has inspired in
our officials, Cardinal Pecci's concessions will be mere matters of form.
He will give way just to the extent that would be expected from a man
of the world, and no more. He is very strongly attached to the Holy
See, and his principles are unbending. A man of his invincible, almost
aggressive, firmness will not yield. He is distinctly one of those priests
who compel admiration. He has considerable political talent, and his
knowledge is still more extensive."

"Cardinal Pecci does not condescend to small compromises. When
we took possession of his seminary, he merely replied that he needed
only a few rooms, and he is now living in his palace with the pupils
from the seminary. He has them to dine and spend the evening with
him. He is doing for Perugia what Cardinal Riario-Sforza tried to do
for Naples : he is creating a scientific movement. In the meantime, not
one of our officials has been invited to cross his threshold. If he
should encounter me, I feel sure he would run away as if he had seen
the devil."

These details, given by a man who certainly cannot be
accused of preconceived admiration for the Bishop of Perugia,
show how great was Mgr. Pecci's care for his young clergy.
He was greatly assisted by his brother Joseph, who had been
compelled by bad health to leave the Society of Jesus for a
time, and whom he had appointed lecturer on theology. Mgr.
Pecci remodelled the whole curriculum of the seminary,
and brought it into conformity with the unassailable and

admirable doctrine of St. Thomas Aquinas. To make sure that his plans were properly carried out by the professors and pupils, he decided to live as much as possible amongst them. He connected his palace with the seminary by means of a sort of bridge, which he used to cross nearly every day, sometimes to be present in one of the class-rooms, and sometimes to mingle with the students during recreation hours. It is related that one of the teaching staff, Signor Brunelli, once arrived at his class-room a few minutes late, and, to his great discomfiture, found his place occupied by the Bishop in person. From that day Signor Brunelli's punctuality left nothing to be desired. Mgr. Pecci's frequent attendance at the seminary was an excellent stimulus, and helped both Bishop and clergy to know each other—the most essential condition for the maintenance of that good understanding necessary for the proper administration of a diocese. The clergy of Perugia could have been held up as an example to those of other Italian dioceses, although all its members were not equally inspired by zeal for the saving of souls. It will be remembered how Mgr. Pecci found himself obliged to take vigorous measures with regard to certain undutiful priests. As a rule, a warning was sufficient to bring back the erring ecclesiastic to the right path. Mgr. Pecci's warnings, in fact, were of a kind seldom requiring repetition. He learnt one day that a certain vicar in his diocese was in the habit of confining his services towards his parishioners to the mere celebration of mass on Sundays. He was never seen in the place from Monday morning until Saturday night, the parish being left six days out of seven to the care of an old priest.

The Bishop paid a surprise visit to the parish, and made his
way into the church, where the old priest was preparing to
begin the service. The Bishop took his place, offered the
Sacrament, preached a sermon to the great edification of the
congregation, and returned to Perugia, still *incognito.* When
the vicar arrived on the following Sunday he was told of the
occurrence. He asked for a description of the unknown
preacher, and had little difficulty in identifying him as the
Bishop. The lesson given with such delicacy and originality
had its effect. The vicar hurried to ask pardon at the episcopal feet, and was never again guilty of a breach of his
residential obligation.

Mgr. Pecci set his clergy a constant example of industry.
As M. Leroy-Beaulieu remarks, " the Pontiff has done little
more than carry out what the Bishop of Perugia conceived
among the mountains of Umbria." Mgr. Pecci's pastoral
letters, in fact, contained the germs of nearly all the
numerous encyclicals that have excited the admiration of the
Christian world by their unimpeachable style and sound
doctrine. The most remarkable of these pastoral letters
are those written in 1876 on " The Church in the Nineteenth
Century," and in 1877 on " The Church and Civilization."
To these must be added Mgr. Pecci's splendid essay, composed in 1860, in favour of the temporal sovereignty of the
Pope, and his masterly reply (1863) to Renan, who had scandalized the Catholic world by devoting his great literary
talents to a misrepresentation of Christ. Mgr. Pecci's
letters on " Popular Errors in regard to Religion " (1864),
" The Conduct of the Clergy in the Present Day " (1866),

and "The Christian Conflict" (1868) should also be mentioned.

The Bishop did not disdain to leave the heights of doctrine in order to discuss certain every-day questions which afforded little scope for literary display. In 1852 he showed his constant desire for the welfare of the poor by

The Vatican gardens—the *Roccolo*.

publishing a set of rules for the management of the Monte di Pietà, or State pawnbroking system. The same desire inspired his important encyclical on the social question—a Pontifical act of incalculable importance, which earned him the title of the workmen's Pope. To return to Perugia, Mgr. Pecci founded in that city a great number of charitable institutions—a boys' orphanage, a home for female penitents, a women's almshouse, an apprentices' association, a benevolent society in aid of indigent priests, etc. His love for the poor was only equalled by his zeal for the house of God. He could not bear to see a place of worship too unfit to be the abode of the Divine Majesty. He restored the cathedral,

Entrance to the private garden of Leo XIII.

built nearly forty churches, and erected a sanctuary, dedicated to Our Lady of Compassion, at the Ponte della Pietra, near Perugia. He completed what he had already done for the instruction of the young clergy by founding the Academy of St. Thomas Aquinas. This establishment was specially intended for the refutation of current errors, whether in

philosophy or theology, and the Bishop frequently taught
in it.

Mgr. Pecci's labours kept him almost constantly at
Perugia. He left it only when the affairs of his diocese
summoned him to Rome, or when his health required change
of air. In 1876, however, he made a rather long stay at
Sinigaglia, during the seaside season, and became acquainted,
under somewhat singular circumstances, with Mgr. Clari, the
future Nuncio at Paris, recently deceased. Cardinal Pecci
was the guest of Mgr. Aggarbati, the Bishop of Sinigaglia.
This prelate's style of hospitality was peculiar to himself.
He gave up one of the best suites of rooms in his palace to
the Cardinal, but gave him clearly to understand that he
would not be provided with food! One of the Vicars General
who resided in the palace, and had observed his Bishop's
singular breach of hospitality, endeavoured to atone for it
as far as lay in his power by devoting himself to Mgr. Pecci,
organizing fêtes in his honour, and accompanying him on
long walks, in the course of which the Cardinal was led to
give full expression to his views on the government of the
Church. "May your Eminence soon have an opportunity
of carrying out plans from which Christianity would derive
so much benefit!" said the Vicar General one day. This
allusion to the high distinction of which he had probably
dreamed did not displease the Bishop, who had already
formed a most favourable opinion of the Vicar General.
Two years afterwards Cardinal Pecci ascended the throne
of St. Peter, and the Vicar General became Bishop of Amelia,

afterwards Bishop of Viterbo, and finally Nuncio in France, a post which, but for his premature death, would have led to his promotion to the Roman purple. Mgr. Aggarbati did not survive the election of Leo XIII.

On returning to Perugia, Mgr. Pecci was informed of the death of Cardinal Antonelli. The event probably caused him little sorrow. Cardinal Antonelli possessed great influence over Pius IX, and neither shared Mgr. Pecci's views nor liked him. This influence was exerted to keep Mgr. Pecci away from the Pontifical Court, and as it had become customary in diplomatic circles to give the Pope the credit of Cardinal Antonelli's personal dislikes, many people really believed that Pius IX "could not endure" Mgr. Pecci, and that the latter reciprocated the feeling. This legend has survived both Pius IX and Cardinal Antonelli, and it will probably not die out with Leo XIII. It has given birth to a variety of unfounded stories industriously circulated for interested motives by adversaries of the Pontifical policy. One of the most characteristic of these anecdotes relates to Mgr. Pecci's promotion in the cardinalate. Pius IX was reported to have announced this promotion to Mgr. Pecci in the following terms :—"Monsignor, I have decided to summon you to the Senate of the Church. I feel sure this will be the first act of my Pontificate that you will not feel called upon to criticize." It has also been asserted that the Pope's sole object in appointing Cardinal Pecci camerlengo,[1]

---

[1] The cardinal who presides over the apostolic assembly, and holds authority in matters temporal during the interval between the death of a Pope and the election of his successor.—Trans.

which he did on the 21st September, 1877, was to prevent
the Cardinal's elevation to the Sovereign Pontificate. During
the interregnum the camerlengo is liable to create a good
deal of discontent amongst the members of the Sacred
College, and, consequently, to diminish his own chance of
succeeding the defunct Pontiff. Pius IX was not so
Machiavelian. It is quite true that Mgr. Pecci, who desired
to obtain a post in or near Rome as a change from the
climate of Perugia, had been unable to obtain either the
bishopric of Albano or the office of datary.[1] This double
failure, however, was the work of Cardinal Antonelli. It is
none the less a fact that, on the death of Cardinal Barnabo,
Prefect of the Propaganda, in 1874, Pius IX thought of
appointing Cardinal Pecci to the vacancy.

"How am I to replace Cardinal Barnabo?" the Pope
asked an English prelate.

"It seems to me, your Holiness, that there is at least one
successor of great merit to be found in the Sacred College."

"Whom do you mean?"

"His Eminence Cardinal Pecci."

"You are quite right," replied the Pope.

Cardinal Antonellli, however, was on the alert, and Mgr.
Pecci remained at Perugia.

After the Cardinal's death Pius IX was free to do justice
to Mgr. Pecci, with the result that the Bishop of Perugia
handed his diocese over to his coadjutor, Mgr. Laurenzi, and

---

[1] An official of the Papal Chancellor's department, so called because
one of his principal functions formerly was to record the date on which
petitions were received.—Trans.

took up his abode in Rome at the Falconieri Palace as camerlengo. This version of the appointment is more credible and does more honour to Pius IX. Towards the end of his reign the "Syllabus Pope" realized that his policy of no compromise would have to give place to something different. Speaking to Mgr. Ferrata (then nunciates' auditor, afterwards Nuncio at Paris and now Cardinal), the Pope said —" I know there must be a change, but it will have to be left to my successor. I cannot break with the traditions of my reign." Is it altogether improbable that Pius IX saw in Mgr. Pecci the successor destined to change the direction of the policy of the Holy See in conformity with the views of Providence, or that he summoned the Cardinal to Rome in order to facilitate, rather than to hinder, his accession? In any case, the appointment—all the more important in view of the fact that the Conclave was known to be close at hand —was received with the utmost favour both in political and religious circles. Signor Bonghi, the Italian ex-Minister of Ecclesiastical Affairs, undoubtedly expressed the general opinion prevailing among statesmen in the following passage in his book *Pius IX and the Future Pope*:—" Cardinal Pecci, the newly-appointed camerlengo, is undoubtedly one of the most distinguished intellects in the Sacred College. He is by nature moderate, and he is one of the most vigorous cardinals in regard to health. He has studied deeply, is a good manager, and was a bishop of great merit. His ideal of a cardinal is as high as any one's, and he has realized it in his own person." Mgr. Pecci was soon to realize his ideal of a Pope, even more completely and unmistakably.

CHAPTER VIII

CARDINAL PECCI AS CAMERLENGO

Appointment, duties, and privileges of the camerlengo—The Government's claims—Bull of 10th October—Deaths of Victor Emanuel and Pius IX—The Holy See vacant—Cardinal Pecci in power—The Novendiales—A diplomatic note—Preparations for the Conclave.

"To manage the property of the Church, to keep watch over the doings of the city magistrates, to provide for the safety of the State, to keep up the military forces of the Holy See, to be ready for war and maintain peace, to have special regard to money, which is the sinew of all public affairs."

As far back as the days of Pius II, these were the duties of the camerlengo. He is the permanent head of the financial department of the Apostolic See. With the single exception of the Chancellor, he is the only dignitary of the Sacred College whose appointment is formally submitted to the cardinals assembled in consistory. When the name is announced, the Pope consults the cardinals by the traditional *Quid vobis videtur?* This, however, is purely a matter of form. The Pope, without waiting for an answer, begins the customary address, concluding with the solemn words—"By

authority of the all-powerful God and of the Apostles Peter
and Paul we entrust the office of camerlengo of the Holy
Church to Cardinal ——, and we hereby invest him *for life*
with all the duties, privileges, and powers laid down in the
apostolic bulls. In the name of the Father, and of the Son,
and of the Holy Ghost."

On the day following his appointment in the manner just
described, the new dignitary receives the staff of office from
the Pope. This ceremony takes place in the presence of the
Apostolic Chamber and the entire Papal Court. The Pope,
seated on his throne, makes the investiture with the words
—"Receive this staff in token of thy jurisdiction and thy
authority, and be henceforth the camerlengo of the Holy
Roman Church."

The camerlengo is the only dignitary of the Sacred College
whose authority does not cease to exist with the Pope who
conferred it. And what is more, though the abolition of the
temporal power of the Popes has reduced the importance of
the camerlengo under ordinary circumstances, the political
situation arising from the new conditions imposed on the
Papacy has proportionately increased the honour and peril
attaching to the post during a vacancy in the Holy See. On
the death of Cardinal De Angelis (July 7, 1877) the Italian
Government asserted that it was entitled to inherit the
exceptional prerogatives of the deceased dignitary, on the
ground of "the inclusion of the Apostolic Chamber within
the domains of the State." Writers were not wanting to
support this singular claim, and even a scheme for the occupation of the Vatican on the death of Pius IX was drawn up.

H

Providence and Cardinal Pecci foiled the plot. King Victor
Emanuel died a month before the Pontiff whom he had
despoiled, his death creating a most opportune diversion;
while Cardinal Pecci summoned a committee of cardinals to
define the rights and duties of the camerlengo, the labours of
this committee resulting, on the 10th October, in a Papal

The St. Damaso courtyard in the Vatican.

Bull calculated to destroy some of the illusions cherished
by the Italian Government.

Victor Emanuel was summoned to his last account on
the 10th January, 1878, "by Him on whom all empires
depend," as Bossuet finely says. On the 7th February, God
recalled to Himself the noble and pure soul of Pius IX. On
the morning of that day, Cardinal Pecci took up his quarters

at the Vatican, so as to be able to cope at once with the
great and responsible duties about to devolve upon him.   He
performed these duties with an authoritativeness, activity,
and energy which afforded no encouragement to resistance.

The Vatican gardens—the Leonine tower.

As soon as he was officially informed of the Pope's death by
the Secretary of State, Cardinal Pecci summoned the prelates
of the Apostolic Chamber, and instructed one of them to
take possession of the Pope's apartments and to draw up an
inventory of their contents.   He then ordered the Vatican

to be cleared of all outsiders, and after having caused every drawer and receptacle for papers to be locked and the keys to be given to him, he proceeded, with the other prelates, to the death chamber. It was then about eight o'clock in the evening. The major-domo and the chief usher of the confidential *camerieri* were already in attendance, while the penitents of St. Peter knelt near the bed, reciting the burial service and the penitential psalms. Robed in violet—the cardinals' mourning colour—without his camail, and his rochet covered by a purple mantle, Cardinal Pecci approached the lifeless body of Pius IX. No hand had yet touched the remains. The face was concealed from view by a white veil. Cardinal Pecci knelt on a violet cushion, whispered a short prayer, and rose to verify the Pope's demise. Meanwhile the attendant valets had reverently uncovered the visage of the august deceased. Three times the camerlengo touched the icy forehead with his silver mallet. Three times his voice broke the silence—"John! John! John!" Turning towards those present, Cardinal Pecci announced—"The Pope is dead." Then he recited the *De Profundis* and performed the aspersion. The chief usher removed the Fisherman's ring from the dead Pope's finger and handed the ring to the camerlengo, in token of the temporary transfer of the authority of the Holy See. A kneeling prothonotary read the official record of the Pope's death, the identification of his remains, and the transfer of the ring to the camerlengo. At the close of this patriarchally simple but awe-inspiring ceremony Cardinal Pecci withdrew to an adjoining room, whence he immediately forwarded telegrams officially announcing the news to the cardinals, and despatches containing his instructions with regard to the Conclave. The death of Pius IX was made known to the public by a notice, signed by the Cardinal Vicar, posted on the doors of all the churches in Rome. The members of the diplomatic body were informed of the event by letters from the Secretary of State.

In the meantime Cardinal Pecci, acting in virtue of his position as head of the executive during the vacancy in the Holy See, appointed the prelates of the Apostolic Chamber to various important posts, such as those of guardians of the datarium, secretarial offices, chancellery, library, archives, and seals; superintendents of the staff, gardens, museums, stables, and offices. His control extended to every department. From the death of Pius IX on the 7th February, to the end of the Conclave on the 20th of the same month, Cardinal Pecci kept the management of every department of the Holy See in his own hands. With his thoughtful but decided and commanding mien, manifesting the conscious superiority of the future Pope, Cardinal Pecci seemed as if already installed, and many of the cardinals were compelled to inwardly admit that in him they had found their master.

In view of the serious nature of the situation, Cardinal Pecci did not hesitate to break with sundry venerable traditions so as to better ensure public order and complete freedom from interference with the Conclave. With these two objects in view, he took upon himself to make an important alteration in the funeral ceremony. Instead of being taken to the Sistine Chapel, and placed to lie in state

throughout the night, the body of Pius IX was conveyed
directly to St. Peter's, at seven o'clock in the evening of the
9th February. The gathering of a crowd, attracted by the
presence of the police, was thus avoided. The procession
traversed the Raphael galleries and the ducal and royal
rooms, but instead of entering the Cathedral, where the Italian
police were on duty, it made its way to the Chapel of the Holy
Sacrament, the railings of which had been previously closed.
The canons of the Cathedral were awaiting the funeral
procession in this chapel, and at ten o'clock the following
morning the first of the nine services, or Novendiales, ordered
by Gregory XV. was celebrated. The omission of the lying-
in-state at night in the Sistine Chapel was of special
importance in regard to the date of the Conclave. It gained
a day, and Cardinal Pecci managed to gain another. Out of
the nine services, six devolve upon the canons of St. Peter's,
and the last three upon the cardinals. The camerlengo
ordered that the first six services should be performed by the
canons alone, in their choir, and that the second series should
be carried out by the cardinals in the Sistine Chapel instead
of the Cathedral, the first service of the second series to
coincide with the last of the first series. This innovation
caused a considerable sensation in the political world, but
Cardinal Pecci remained unmoved. He was quite aware of
the extent of his rights and duties, and he was fully resolved
neither to abandon the one nor neglect the other. Moreover,
he did not take the responsibility of deciding on any really
important point without previously consulting the Novendial
congregations, as the meetings held by the cardinals present

Mgr. Pecci at the death-bed of Pius IX.

in Rome during the period between the death of the Pope
and the opening of the Conclave are called. Formerly the
first of these Novendiales did not take place until three days
after the Pope's death. Cardinal Pecci, however, summoned
this first assembly to meet on the day after the decease of
Pius IX. This proceeding was distinctly clever. It had the
double advantage of securing the camerlengo the good graces
of the electorate, and diminishing the importance of the
private meetings of the three heads of orders—cardinals,
bishops, priests, and deacons—who, with the camerlengo,
constitute the executive body during the vacancy in the
Holy See.

The first of the Novendiales was almost entirely devoted
to a reading of the various Pontifical ordinances in regard
to Conclaves, such as the *In eligendis* Bull by Pius IV
(October 1, 1562) and the *Æterni Patris* Bull by Gregory XV
(Nov. 15, 1621). These two Papal deliverances contain a
carefully-codified set of rules still in force at the election of
Popes. Among the most interesting of these regulations are
the following :—

"In Eligendis" Bull.

1. Cardinals absent from the place at which the Pope's
death may take place shall be awaited ten days, during which
period the obsequies of the deceased Pontiff shall be
carried out.

2. At the end of the ten days the cardinals shall enter
into Conclave. They shall immediately proceed to elect a

Pope, without delaying this the principal business of the Conclave by drawing up capitulations or conditions to be imposed on the future Pope. A ballot shall be taken every day, and, after the first, it is permissible to employ that form of voting known as the *accessit*, which permits of votes being

Pio Centra, valet of Leo XIII.

immediately registered in favour of any candidate who may have obtained votes at the first ballot.

5. During the vacancy, the College of Cardinals shall have no jurisdiction and no legislative, administrative, or executive power. All rights and privileges of the Pontifical jurisdiction shall be reserved for the future Pope.

7. The powers of the camerlengo shall remain in force during the vacancy.

10. The chambers or cells used by the cardinals at the Conclave shall be apportioned by lot.

Bedchamber of Leo XIII in the Leonine tower.

11. Except those persons appointed by the canons, no one shall be allowed to remain either in or near the Conclave, and still less in the rooms above or below.

The walled partition at the entrance to the Conclave shall

be regularly inspected by the cardinals appointed for that purpose. They shall also see that no hole, fissure, or other secret opening of any kind has been made in the walls, floors, or ceilings.

14. The officials admitted to the Conclave or to communicate with its members shall be as follows :—a sacristan with one attendant ; two masters of ceremonies ; a confessor of the Conclave ; a secretary of the Sacred College ; two physicians, a surgeon, a chemist, and two assistants ; a carpenter, a master mason, and a barber with two assistants ; and eight or ten servants for general attendance upon the Conclave, such servants to have been chosen by secret ballot by the Sacred College.

15. As soon as the Conclave is formed no one shall be allowed to converse at the entrance. Such permission shall be given to ambassadors themselves for urgent reasons only.

16. All communication with persons outside the Conclave, either by words, signs, or letters sent or received, is forbidden.

17. All bets relating to the election of the Sovereign Pontiff shall be null and void.

18. No cardinal shall benefit by food prepared for any other. Each shall take his food in his own room. Each meal shall consist of a single course.

19. The prelates entrusted with the guardianship of the Conclave shall, under penalty of ecclesiastical interdiction, most carefully examine the food brought into the Conclave, as well as every other person or thing passing in or out, so that letters, notes, etc., can neither be brought in nor taken out.

21. No cardinal who has not reached deacon's orders shall take part in the election.

22. The cardinals are most earnestly exhorted to have God alone before their eyes. They should silence all passions and tread all worldly interests under-foot. They should ignore the solicitations of princes. They should abstain from party spirit, trickery, and fraud, and especially from all illicit contracts, compromises, agreements, or engagements. They should avoid disclosing their votes. They are forbidden to stir up tumults or to bring about delay in the election.

25. In order to avoid conflicts and schisms, it is hereby laid down that no ecclesiastical censure or excommunication shall prevent a cardinal from exercising his right to vote at the election of a Pope.

26. The terms of this Bull shall be observed in whatever place the Conclave may be held, whether Rome or elsewhere.

"ÆTERNI PATRIS" BULL.

1. The election of the Sovereign Pontiff shall take place only in secret conclave.

2. No election shall be valid unless supported by a majority of at least two-thirds of the voters.

3. The ordinary form of election requires that there shall be a ballot and written voting papers.

4. Any electoral session which may not have produced a definite result at the first ballot shall be completed by a second ballot, or *accessit*.

5. In no ballot shall any cardinal vote for himself.

6. No candidate shall be considered elected until after the announcement of all the votes. In the event of a candidate receiving exactly two-thirds of the total number of votes, that part of the papers containing the voter's signature [1] shall be opened, in order to make sure that the candidate has not voted for himself.

12. Should an *accessit* ballot be necessary, the same precautions shall be taken with a view to preserving the secrecy of the voting. Electors who, at such second ballot, desire for the same candidate as before, can merely employ the formula, "*Accedo nemini.*"

18. Three scrutineers shall be chosen by lot among the

---

[1] "The voting papers," says Lucius Lector in his remarkable work, *The Conclave,* "are so contrived as to maintain the secrecy of the ballot, while at the same time permitting an examination of the papers in case of need. The papers are prepared beforehand, general directions being printed on them. They are divided into three compartments, in the lowest of which the elector inscribes any device or cypher. The top compartment, which is unsealed only in extreme cases, contains the voter's name: *Ego cardinalis* ——. The middle compartment contains the candidate's name with the following formula: *Eligo in summum pontificem R. D. meum D. card.* ——. The paper is folded so that only the middle compartment is visible, the other two being turned under and sealed with a fancy seal of no particular design, so as to give no clue to the voter's identity. For additional security, so that nothing shall be seen of the contents through the paper, the back of the upper and lower compartments is covered with vignettes and arabesques. The words *nomen* and *signa* are also printed in large letters on the back so as to prevent the scrutineers from inadvertently opening the paper." The shape of the voting papers as thus described by Lucius Lector, and the usual way of filling them up, folding, sealing, and counting them, are in strict conformity with the provisions of articles 9 and 10 of the *Æterni Patris* Bull.

cardinals to count the votes. Three revisers shall also be appointed by lot to check the scrutineers. The voting papers shall afterwards be burnt in the presence of the whole Conclave.

19. The ballots shall take place twice daily; in the morning after Mass, and in the evening after the singing of the *Veni Creator*. All cardinals must attend these services, under penalty of excommunication.

20. The cardinals are most strictly forbidden to enter into any compact or agreement, or to give any promise or undertaking. All threats or signals of any kind, whether written or spoken, intended to bring about the inclusion or exclusion of any person or persons through the giving or refusal of votes, are also strictly forbidden, but these provisions shall not exclude any proper exchange of views or understanding with a view to the election of the Sovereign Pontiff.

21. The election shall be null and void—

    a. When not conducted in closed conclave.

    b. When no candidate shall have received a majority of two-thirds of the votes, his own excluded.

    c. When it is effected by a compromise [1] without the unanimous consent of all the cardinals present, or when the cardinal so elected shall have voted in his own favour.

---

[1] The election by compromise is effected by the cardinals unanimously appointing a certain number of their colleagues to select the Pope. This appointment is recorded in a special form laid down by Gregory XV, indicating the conditions under which the delegates are to vote and the procedure agreed upon to establish the validity of such vote.—Lucius Lector in *The Conclave.*

The second Novendiale took place on the 9th February in the consistory room. The locality of the Conclave was the principal subject discussed, and Rome was decided upon by thirty-two votes against five. At the next meeting, held on the following day, the reading of the apostolic regulations for the election was completed, the seals were removed, and two cardinals were appointed to deliver the funeral oration over Pius IX and the opening speech at the Conclave. At this meeting the camerlengo reported that the Secretary of State, Cardinal Simeoni, had already instructed one of the architects of the apostolic palaces to prepare two plans for the accommodation of the Conclave. The first of these plans was to utilize the canonry and sacristy of the cathedral; the second was to fit up premises for the Conclave in the Vatican itself. The first of these plans was immediately rejected. The other was referred to a committee consisting of Cardinals Di Pietro, Simeoni, Sacconi, and Borromeo. The committee's labours were so actively pushed on by the camerlengo that they were completed the same day. The second plan was adopted, and the work was begun on the following morning. At the fourth Novendiale, the 18th February was fixed as the date of the Conclave. At the fifth meeting Cardinal Franchi, afterwards one of the Grand Electors, read a diplomatic note drafted by himself at the request of the camerlengo. This note, which drew the attention of the Powers to the exceptional conditions under which the Conclave was about to be held, was unanimously approved, save that one cardinal did not vote. It was signed on the 16th February by the camerlengo and the three heads of orders, and was transmitted on the 19th to the members of the diplomatic body.

Cardinal Pecci was convinced that "to govern is to foresee." He left no stone unturned to provide against all possible contingencies. Whilst he was taking diplomatic measures to avoid all interference with the Conclave, several cardinals, who were strongly in favour of his election, began to influence public opinion in that direction. Cardinals Franchi and Bartolini, for instance, distributed specially written pamphlets on the needs of the Church. Fully realizing the influence of the Press in a question exciting as much interest in the political as in the religious world, they "inspired" sundry newspapers. Traces of this more or less mysterious "inspiration" might easily be found in the files of the *Times*, the *Manchester Guardian*, the *Neue Freie Presse*, the *Figaro*, the *Fanfulla*, the *Gazzetta d'Italia*, the *Corriere della Sera*, etc. It is only justice to point out that the example was set by the Italian Government. Moreover, the Quirinal has not abandoned a practice, the advantages of which it has often realized. Signor Nicotera, the Premier, informed the members of the Press during the session of the Chamber on the 22nd January, 1892, that a special Vatican information bureau had been opened for their accommodation at the Ministry of the Interior—a thoughtful attention that was not left altogether unrewarded.

That worldly preparations were made, as on previous occasions, for the 1878 Conclave, is certain. It could not well be otherwise, seeing that the preparations were made by men ; but human designs are not necessarily in contradiction

I

of those of Providence.   Experience shows that God makes
light, when it pleases Him, both of ordinary calculations and
deep political combinations.   When the princes of the Church
are called upon to perform the responsible duty of giving that
Church a new head, its members should believe that the
Spirit exerts its silent influence within the mind of every
elector, so that the Pope, designated by the majority of the
Sacred College, is in reality the elect of God.

PART II

CHAPTER I

ELECTION AND CORONATION

Cost of a vacancy in the Holy See—Innovations at the 1878 Conclave
—An economical camerlengo—Mgr. Ricci—The first ballots—Electoral
intrigues—Cardinal Pecci's frame of mind—His election—Obedience—
The benediction *urbi et orbi*—The triple tiara.

THE 1878 Conclave differed from its predecessors in the
abolition of separate cells for the cardinals, and the inclusion of
every floor of the Pontifical palace within the area shut off
for the proceedings. All the arrangements had to be made
afresh, the previous Conclave, which resulted in the election
of Pius IX, having been held in the Quirinal. What, it may
be asked, had become of the scaffolding, planks, and hangings
which were used on that occasion, and were no doubt put
aside for use at future Conclaves? No one knows, but in any
event there can be little surprise at the disappearance of
these mute witnesses of the commencement of so long a reign
—so exceptionally long as to demolish the legend that no
Pope can hope to "see Peter's years" (*non videbis annos
Petri*). If this unpleasant prophecy really formed part of the

115

coronation ceremony, Pius IX would have been still more justified than Benedict XIV in making the witty reply attributed, on doubtful evidence, to that prelate : *Hoc non est de fide* (" That is not an article of faith ").

To return to the arrangements for the 1878 Conclave, the spacious halls of the Vatican were divided into sets of small apartments, each containing three or four rooms separated by mere partitions. In this way a set of rooms was provided for every member of the Sacred College, and every cardinal was able to have his "conclavist" and servant at hand. The consistory hall, on the second floor, was set apart for the meetings of the full Conclave. The first-floor rooms in the Gregory XIII wing, under the clock pavilion, were devoted to meetings of committees and various congregations. The kitchens [1] were fitted up on the ground floor of the same wing, and the other subordinate offices were installed in the premises of the Palazzo Vecchio, in the vicinity of the Sistine Chapel. The work carried out under Signor Martinucci's plans cost exactly 57,871 lire 67 centimes. To this sum should be added 20,000 lire paid to another architect, Signor

---

[1] Kitchens were used for the first time within the precincts of the Conclave in 1878. On previous occasions the cardinals' meals were prepared outside and brought in gala carriage. These culinary processions with their "dapifer" seneschal, flanked by a cup-bearer and an equerry, used to form one of the curiosities of old Rome. Notwithstanding all this display, the dishes were carefully examined by the guardians of the "rotas," who were instructed to see that no illicit missives were concealed in the food. At the 1878 Conclave Cardinal von Hohenlohe was the only member of the Sacred College who had his meals brought from outside. It is needless to say that this solitary exception excited a good deal of comment.

Vespignani, for fitting up the Sistine Chapel for the ballots. The total cost of the vacancy in the Holy See amounted, in round figures, to £6000—a comparatively small sum. In former times the expenses usually exceeded £20,000, and sometimes reached double that amount.

The camerlengo effected considerable savings in other directions. He reduced the gratuity usually paid to the Conclave attendants from 15,000 to 5850 crowns. He flatly refused Signor Martinucci a special gratuity of 1000 crowns, and strongly objected to satisfy the claims of the discontented Swiss Guards. "These usages are abuses," was his invariable reply when tradition was pleaded; and he had his own way.

The Conclave[1] opened on the 18th February with the Mass of the Holy Spirit, sung by Cardinal Schwartzenberg in the Pauline Chapel, and with the oration *pro eligendo pontifice*, delivered in the Sistine Chapel by Mgr. Mercurelli, secretary to Pius IX. All the cardinals in Rome attended

Mgr. Angell, private secretary to Leo XIII.

[1] Only five members of the Conclave which elected Leo XIII now survive—Cardinals Oreglia di Santo-Stephano and Parocchi, of the order of bishops; Ledochowski and Canossa, of the order of priests; and Mertel, of the order of deacons.

this double ceremony. These cardinals were much more numerous than at the previous Conclave. Among them were twenty-five foreigners, whilst the Romans alone took part in the election of Pius IX. It is, too, probable that the international element will be more and more strongly represented in future Conclaves; firstly, because of the growing facility of communication between Rome and distant places; and secondly, because the Sacred College is becoming more open to nations other than Italy. Pius IX increased the number of cardinals not living in Rome, and during the Pontificate of Leo XIII their number has sometimes almost equalled that of the Roman cardinals. Thus is the catholicity of the Church becoming more and more pronounced, in accordance with the will of the Divine Founder.

After the Mass of the Holy Spirit, the members of the Sacred College separated. They met again at half-past four in the afternoon in the Pauline Chapel, whence they walked in procession, to the chanting of the *Veni Creator*, to the Sistine Chapel. Here the apostolic regulations for the election of the Pope were again read to them, and they took the customary oath. The camerlengo then administered the oath to Prince Chigi, Marshal of the Palace, his four officers, his gentleman-in-waiting, steward, chaplain, and secretary; the officers of the Swiss Guard, Palatine Guard, and gendarmerie of the apostolic palaces; and finally to the ecclesiastical attendants, the bishop sacristan, and the ushers, who formerly, if certain chroniclers of the reign of Pius VIII are to be believed, used to enjoy anything but a good reputation.

One prelate thought himself entitled to dispense with the formality of taking the oath. This prelate was Mgr. Ricci, the major-domo, who used to be called "the Pope's eyeball" during the lifetime of Pius IX, in reference to the confidence and affection with which the Pontiff regarded him. Mgr. Ricci was prostrated by grief at the death of his master and had fallen ill.

"The major-domo is extremely unwell, your Eminence," Mgr. Pecci was told when he expressed surprise at Mgr. Ricci's absence.

"Then let him get up and come! I want him!" was the imperious reply. Mgr. Ricci was obliged to obey and make his appearance, pale, wasted, and shivering with fever.

Mgr. Mazzolini, private chaplain to Leo XIII.

The superficial observer might conclude from this incident that Leo XIII is hard-hearted. The fact is that every man designated by Providence to command other men is naturally inclined to regard them first of all as instruments of his own will. So absorbed is he in his work, that he often sacrifices his tools. This is neither just nor charitable, but the really great man always knows how to atone for whatever injury he may have inflicted in the interest of his own higher purposes. Immediately after his elevation to the chair of St. Peter, Leo XIII sent for Mgr. Ricci and said to him — "I have hurt your feelings,

Monsignor, and I beg your pardon." He reappointed
Mgr. Ricci major-domo of the apostolic palaces, and soon
afterwards summoned him to the Senate of the Church.

On the 18th February, at half-past five in the afternoon,
the Conclave was finally separated from the outer world.
The ringing of a small bell, and the repetition of the formula
"Extra omnes!" by the Master of the Ceremonies, was the
signal for all outsiders to retire. All the outlets had already
been walled up, with the exception of the great door of the
Sala Regia, through which the last of the crowd passed out
at about seven o'clock. The camerlengo, accompanied by the
three heads of orders, then went through all the rooms by
torchlight to make sure that communication between the two
hundred and fifty persons shut up in the Vatican and the rest
of the world was impossible, except through the four rotas, or
small receptacles turning on pivots. These rotas, contrived
for the admission of provisions and official correspondence,
were placed under the watchful care of prelates of the
apostolic chamber, the prothonotaries, the bishops, and the
prelates of the signature.

The first ballot began, after mass, at half-past nine on the
following morning. In accordance with the regulation, all
the cardinals were clad in an ample violet robe of woollen
material, with a plaited sleeveless cape lying flat on the
shoulders. This robe, which has no sleeves, is fastened at
the chest with a hook, and ends in a long train. On their
way to the Sistine Chapel, the cardinals passed through the
Sala Regia, with its splendid frescoes by Vasari and Della
Porta, representing Pepin and Charlemagne offering presents

to the head of the Church, Peter of Aragon laying his
sovereignty in homage at the feet of Innocent III, Gregory
VII absolving Henry IV of Germany at Canossa, the recon-
ciliation of Frederick Barbarossa with Alexander III in St.
Mark's Square, Venice, the battle of Lepanto, and the return
to Rome of Gregory XI, the last of the Avignon Popes.

. An altar had been erected in the Sistine Chapel, below
Michael Angelo's *Last Judgment*. On this altar was the
silver-gilt chalice in which each cardinal was to deposit his
voting-paper. At the foot of the altar was a table for the
examination of the papers. . Close at hand were the cardinals'
stalls, arranged in a semi-circle and surmounted by canopies,
which emblems of sovereignty were to be taken down as soon
as the new Pope's name was announced. In front of each stall
was a small table for convenience in filling up, folding, and
sealing the forms. Near the altar was the open grate for
burning the papers after each ballot. To the right and left
of the entrance were two dressing-rooms, one containing
white vestments for the future Pontiff. Cassocks of various
sizes were of course kept here, so that whoever the new Pope
might be, he would find a garment to fit him.

When the cardinals—each preceded by his attendant
carrying the portfolio and inkstand—had reached the chapel,
the bishop sacristan recited the ritual prayers. The Master
of the Ceremonies proclaimed the order " Extra omnes ! "
and the electors were left to themselves. A cardinal bolted
the door, and the election began. The first ballot resulted
in twenty-three votes being cast for Cardinal Pecci. At the
second, which took place in the evening of the same

day, he received twenty-six, and then thirty-eight, an accessory ballot being taken. He was still three votes short of the required majority, but his election on the following day appeared to be a certainty, in spite of the opposition of Cardinals Randi, Bilio, and Oreglia, who acted as faction leaders against him.[1] Cardinal Randi made persistent but unavailing efforts in favour of Cardinal Chigi, while Cardinal Bilio supported the candidature of Cardinal Martinelli, who he declared was "a saint."[2]

"If Martinelli is a saint," replied Mgr. Bartolini, "let him pray for us; but a saint is not what we want at the head of the Church just now." And Cardinal Bartolini went from group to group, expatiating on Mgr. Pecci's qualifications. "He has been a delegate, and he knows the temporal government; he has been a nuncio, and he knows diplomacy; he has been a bishop thirty-two years, and he knows the government of the Church." More than one encounter occurred between Cardinals Randi and

---

[1] The voting is carried out as follows :—Each cardinal, when his name is called, approaches the altar, kneels, rises, and before placing his voting-paper in the chalice, holds the paper above that vessel and utters the following words : "*Testor Christum Dominum, qui me judicaturus est, me eligere quem secundum Deum judico eligi debere, et quod idem in accessu præstabo*" (I call upon Christ our Lord, Who shall judge me, to witness that I vote for him who, I believe before God, ought to be chosen, and that I will do the same at the accessory ballot).

[2] Cardinal Pecci was elected at the third ballot by forty-four votes, or three more than the required majority. When the papers were counted it was seen that one of them bore the words "*Eligo neminis*" (I choose no one). This paper was of course annulled amid general laughter. The identity of the cardinal who had the bad taste to perpetrate this pleasantry is not known.

Bartolini, the former accusing the latter of caballing, which Cardinal Bartolini stoutly denied. Cardinal Oreglia, who was not in favour of Mgr. Pecci's candidature until *after* the election, at first supported Cardinal Bilio; but the latter had no prospect of success when the third ballot opened on the morning of the 20th February, the opponents of Mgr. Pecci having decided, though without much confidence in the result, to support Cardinal Franchi.

And what was passing in the mind of the future Leo XIII during these few momentous hours, so full of influence on his own destiny and the Church's future? Ambitious he was, as he had a right to be, in the highest and best meaning of the word; and it cannot be supposed that he had never dreamed, with secret longing but with secret terror also, of succeeding to the Papacy. With what intensity these two opposing sentiments must have warred within his mind as the still distant prospect drew nearer and nearer! The thought of the terrible responsibilities that might soon devolve upon him caused him indescribable anxiety. He well realized the full extent of these responsibilities, and their crushing weight seemed to him already on his shoulders. A lawyer named Pecorari wrote that his wife, who had recently died, had appeared to him in a dream and declared that Cardinal Pecci would be elected Pope. The cardinal did not even smile at this piece of childish simplicity. He was visibly depressed and excessively nervous. "Don't you know," he said, "what they want of me? I am old and feeble and shall soon succumb. They are giving me death, and not the Papacy."

In his book *Sovereigns, Statesmen, and Churchmen,* Mr. Charles Benoist gives an admirable description of Cardinal Pecci's state of mind on the morning of the memorable 20th February. This passage deserves to be cited in full:—

Mgr. Cagiano di Azevedo, *maître de chambre* to Leo XIII.

"Vainly he tried to take refuge in the past. The quiet old house at Carpineto, the Jesuit College at Viterbo, his ordination, his first appointment, the cardinal's hat itself: how far away all these things seemed! Everything he had

felt and experienced appeared to have forsaken him as
he stood trembling at the threshold of this glorious but
mysterious future, preparing for solitude and knowing how

Private oratory and chapel of Leo XIII.

high he must stand above even those nearest to him. Why
would they not let him finish reciting his verses to his
fellow-students in the olive grove on the slope of the hill
behind St. Peter's in Montorio?

*'Quam flore in primo felix, quam prima Lepinis
Ortu jugis, patrio sub lare, vita fuit!'*

"Yes, that was it: the Garden of Olives. He was there, like Jesus, and they were betraying him and preparing a Calvary for him: the throne! Then he seemed to fall into a slumber and dream that he was clasping the trunk of a poplar, and that the tree grew and grew within his arms until it touched the sky. From time to time he seemed to hear his own name uttered by the dean of the Sacred College. Then the prophecy of St. Malachi recurred to him. Was not Pius IX, *Crux de cruce*, to be succeeded by a Pope who should be *Lumen in cœlo? Lumen in cœlo!* That must be the star on his coat-of-arms! But what was he that he should hope to become the most honoured patriarch and lord, the bishop raised to the apostolic summit, the gatekeeper of the House of God, the head and mouthpiece of the apostolate, the bond of union; to become an Abraham in patriarchal dignity, a Melchisedech in priestly sanctity, a Moses in command, a Samuel in jurisdiction, a Peter in power, and an Anointed like Christ Himself! A mist came before his eyes with every vote added to those already cast for him. In this the evening of his day he saw, not night, but the dawning of eternal day.

"Suddenly he saw the sub-dean prostrate at his feet, and heard the words, 'Acceptas-ne electionem de te canonice factam in summum pontificem?' (Dost thou accept thy due and regular election to the sovereign pontificate?) He remembered Celestin V, and the undying stigma inflicted by Dante, his own favourite poet, on 'the shade of him who

in cowardice uttered the great refusal.' His voice rose to
his lips in almost a sob as he replied, 'Such being God's
will I cannot gainsay it.' 'Under what name wilt thou be
known?' 'As Leo XIII, in remembrance of Leo XII, whom
I have always venerated.' All the canopies save his were
thrown down. They clad him, dazed and barely conscious,
in white:[1] *Lumen in cœlo*, they gave him a garment of light.
They kissed his ring, his feet; they led him where they
would. From the inner loggia of St. Peter's he blessed the
city and the whole world. His tall, wasted form, with arms

---

[1] After the members of the Conclave have removed the newly-elected
Pope's cardinal's robes, they clothe him in white stockings and red
slippers, white cassock, cap and silk girdle, rochet, red velvet or silk
mozetta, and red stole embroidered with gold. When the cardinals
take off his red cap, it is usual for the Pope to take it from them and
place it on the head of the secretary of the Conclave, this post being
always considered as a preliminary to the cardinalate. Owing either
to absence of mind or a desire to give a hint that he did not consider
himself bound by this tradition, Leo XIII quietly put the red cap in
his pocket when it was presented to him. The secretary of the
Conclave, Mgr. Lasagni, was none the less raised to the cardinalate
soon afterwards.

On being led back to the altar on which the voting had taken place,
Leo XIII received the homage of the cardinals, and accomplished the
first act of his Papacy by appointing, as pro-camerlengo, Mgr.
Schwartzenberg, Archbishop of Prague, who placed the Fisherman's
ring on the Pope's finger.

The election was announced at a quarter-past one by Cardinal
Caterini from the balcony of St. Peter's. The bells of every church in
Rome immediately rang out to announce the "tidings of great joy."
Leo XIII gave the benediction *urbi et orbi* from the inner loggia of
St. Peter's. He received, for the second time, the homage of the
cardinals and of the representatives of the Roman patricians, and finally
retired to his apartments at six o'clock.

extended in the act of benediction, was like a living cross.
He was the Vicar of Jesus Christ, the successor of the
Fisher of Men, stretching forth his hands to bless two
hundred million souls."

Every convict, as the saying is, is allowed twenty-four
hours to curse the judge who sentenced him. The cardinals
who had been foremost in opposition to Cardinal Pecci did not
wait so long to express their joy at the judgment the Conclave
had given against them. "This is not an election but a Divine
inspiration," proclaimed Cardinal Ferrieri, who had boasted
only a few hours before of lowering young Pecci's pride by
getting the better of him in debate at the Academy of
Theology. Another opponent, Cardinal Pietro, found a pithy
phrase to express his devotion to Leo XIII. "Ecce nos, os
tuum et caro tua erimus" (We desire to be thy mouth and
thy flesh), he said in his address as sub-dean of the Sacred
College, at the coronation of the new Pope.

On that day, the 3rd March, Leo XIII celebrated Mass in
the Sistine Chapel, at the altar beneath Michael Angelo's great
fresco. As soon as the chair on which he was seated reached
the nave, an usher waved before his eyes a bundle of tow at
the end of a silver staff, and uttered the words, "Pater
Sancte, sic transit gloria mundi." The Church gives this
admirable lesson of humility to its new head at the very
moment of his taking possession of his threefold power,
doctrinal, sacramental, and pastoral, symbolized by the triple
tiara placed on his head by the *doyen* of the cardinal deacons
with the consecrated formula, "Accipe tiaram tribus coronis
ornatam, et scias te esse patrem principum et regum,

rectorem orbis in terra, vicarium salvatoris nostri Jesu
Christi, cui est honor in sæcula sæculorum.   Amen."
(Receive the triple tiara, and know that thou art the father

Waiting-room in the Leonine tower.

of princes and kings, the rector of this world and vicar of our
Saviour Jesus Christ, to whom be all honour for ever and
ever.   Amen.)

K

CHAPTER II

THE VATICAN

THE temporal power of the Pope is now nothing more than a memory and a hope. But it can be easily understood that the exercise of a spiritual power extending over the whole Catholic world necessitates considerable expenditure. Man being made up of mind and body, material means must be used for spiritual effects, and it is only just that those who live for the altar should live by the altar. Therefore the Pope must have a budget. When the Pope was still in reality a temporal prince, the estimates of the Papal States, in addition to his own revenues, provided for a civil list of 600,000 Roman crowns, or 3,225,000 lire. Under the Act of Guarantee, this civil list is now replaced by a perpetual and inalienable *rente* representing a capital of 64,500,000 lire. The Act of Guarantee, however, has never been, and cannot be, recognized by the Holy See. Such recognition would imply acquiescence in the confiscation of the Pope's temporal power, and to this the Papacy can never consent. In consequence, the *rente* is a mere fiction, just as the former civil list is nothing more than a historic souvenir. Nevertheless, Leo

XIII requires a sum of £280,000 every year for the administration of the Church. This expenditure is apportioned as follows:—cardinals and diplomatic representatives, £20,000; maintenance of the Vatican and its dependencies (libraries, museums, etc.), £100,000; Papal charities and subsidies to Catholic schools in Rome, £60,000; presents and grants in aid, £60,000; various expenses, £40,000.

The pay of the little Pontifical army of course comes under the head of maintenance of the Vatican. The sum is comparatively small, the Pontifical army now consisting of only three corps of guards—the Noble Guard, Swiss Guard, and Palatine Guard—and a body of gendarmes. The Swiss Guard alone is a tax upon the Vatican finances. *Pas d'argent, pas de Suisse*, says the proverb. The Noble Guard is drawn entirely from the Roman aristocracy, and the Palatine Guard from the lower middle class. The Noble Guard is under the command of Prince Emilio Altieri, and consists of a colonel, a lieutenant, a sub-lieutenant, eight officers of inferior rank, a cadet, forty-eight guards, a quartermaster, a mounted messenger, four trumpeters, a master-at-arms, and a storekeeper. Admission can only be obtained between the ages of twenty-one and twenty-five. Every candidate for the Noble Guard must belong to a family of at least sixty years' recognized nobility in the Papal States. He must also prove that he has a capital of at least £800, and that his constitution is good. One of the duties of the Noble Guards is to convey to prelates not living in Italy the news of their elevation to the cardinalate, and to hand them the red cap, the first mark of their new dignity.

The Noble Guards cannot marry without the consent of
their commanding officer. They are promoted according to
seniority, except the commandant, who is appointed by the
Pope. Neither the Noble Guards nor the Palatine Guards
live in the Vatican, and they are summoned there for service
only on special occasions. The Swiss Guards, on the other
hand, are quartered in barracks behind the apostolic palaces.
This corps was founded by Julius II, who was Bishop of
Lausanne, and the uniform was designed by Raphael. The
Swiss Guard consists of one hundred officers and men, all tall,
and all natives of Catholic cantons. Their sole duty is to
keep guard at the outer doors and in the corridors of the
Vatican, where their fine appearance make a great impression
on visitors. Their present commandant is Colonel de Courton,
an officer whom the Pope esteems highly. Their pay is only
fifty lire per month, and out of this small sum they have to
provide one meal a day. The gendarmes, who number
one hundred and twenty, are responsible for the maintenance of order in the Vatican. The entire strength of the
Pontifical army thus amounts to six hundred officers and
men—the smallest physical force at the service of the greatest
moral force in the world.

The Vatican income is derived from St. Peter's Patrimony
and St. Peter's Pence—two things which are often confounded
but are essentially distinct. The " patrimony " consists of the
regular revenue derived from investments of capital, from a
small amount of house-property, from the granting of patents
of Pontifical nobility, from registration and other fees charged
on dispensations—especially matrimonial. These receipts

amount to about £40,000 in all. The "pence" are the voluntary contributions of the entire world. A few years ago they totalled £400,000, of which about two-thirds was supplied by France. The income from this source has since, however, considerably fallen off, owing to certain political considerations, the French Monarchists having thought fit to show themselves less generous to Leo XIII in retaliation for the advances he has made to the Republic. On the other hand, St. Peter's Pence was swelled by the numerous offerings sent to the Pope on his priestly jubilee in 1886, and his episcopal jubilee in 1893, amounting to about £1,600,000. At the death of Pius IX there was a reserve fund of something like £1,200,000, amassed by the far-seeing economy of Cardinal Antonelli. Unfortunately Mgr. Folchi, the Secretary of the Committee of Cardinals appointed to manage this capital, conceived the idea of investing it in Italian Government stock, with the object of alleviating the financial crisis from which Rome was suffering. Leo XIII consented to this proposal. The mistake cost him fully £800,000. It should be added, that the Pope's capital is invested abroad, chiefly with Messrs. Rothschild in London, where, by a curious coincidence, King Humbert has also, it is said, deposited his private fortune in safe keeping.

Leo XIII of course uses St. Peter's Pence as he thinks fit. When Cardinal Mocenni, the treasurer or finance minister of the Holy See, requires money, he goes to the Pope, who simply produces the required amount from one of the drawers of his desk. This lack of financial control, however, does not alter the fact that no predecessor of Leo XIII was so careful of the

proper employment of the Pontifical finances. No Pope was
ever less addicted to what is called nepotism. A few years
ago, one of his nephews, who had invested part of his money
in building a villa, was obliged to sell it for half its cost,
in order to meet his engagements. Leo XIII could un-

Doctor Gaetano Mazzoni.

doubtedly have prevented this family trouble. He refused,
not through hardness of heart, but because he does not
consider himself entitled to use the slightest part of the
patrimony of the Holy See on behalf of any interests except
those of the Church. But when those interests are at stake
he does not hesitate. He has, for instance, spent enormous

Private antechamber of Leo XIII.

sums in founding and assisting schools. The Benedictine
College of St. Anselm, which rises majestically on the summit
of the Aventine Hill, cost him nearly £160,000. Among
many other buildings erected or restored by Leo XIII
may be mentioned the Church of Santa Maria Maggiore,
the canonry of St. John Lateran, the Vatican seminary
villa, the institutions at Carpineto, Anagni, etc. He has
given munificent encouragement to art. He subscribed £400
to the fund for erecting the Dante monument at Ravenna.
The painter of the *Holy Family*, a picture intended for the
Turin Exhibition of Christian Art, received £400 from the
Holy Father. To Leo XIII we owe the restoration of the
Sistine Chapel, the world-renowned choirs of which were,
at the time of his accession, by no means equal to their
reputation. By the Pope's order the six Borgia rooms in
the Vatican were magnificently restored. These apartments
(known as the Pontiffs', Mysteries, Saints', Fine Arts, Credo
and Syllabus rooms) are named after the real or imaginary
figures in Pinturicchio's frescoes, and after the Biblical
personages therein represented.

At the entrance to the Pontiffs' room is the following
inscription :—

LEO XIII. P. M.

HAS. ÆDES

CAMERARUM. PICTURIS. INSIGNES

PAVIMENTO. REFECTO

EXCULTIS. ORNATU. VARIO. PARIETIBUS

IN. DIGNITATEM. PRISTINAM

RESTITUIT. ET DEDICAVIT

AN. PONT. XX.

As soon as the restoration of the Borgia rooms was completed, in September 1897, the Pope gave orders for the preparation of a magnificent album of photogravure reproductions of the frescoes. Copies of this album, bound in massive oak boards, with an artistically chiselled hasp bearing the Pontifical arms, were presented to the heads of all the principal states. This album contains a preface by Father Francis Ehrlé, of the Society of Jesus, Prefect of the Vatican Library, and by Commendatore Stevenson, Director of the Vatican Museum of Numismatics. On the first page is the following dedication—which posterity will ratify—to Leo XIII, the "immortal patron of science, literature, and art":—

ALLA SANTITA

DI NOSTRO SIGNORE

LEONE PP. XIII

IMMORTALE FAUTORE

DELLE SCIENZE, DELLE LETTERE E DELLE ARTI

NELL' OCCASIONE IN CHE LE STANZE BORGIA

DALLA SOVRANA MUNIFICENZA DI LUI

SONE RESTITUITE ALL' ANTICO SPLENDORE

GLI AUTORI U. O. D. D.

Though the Pope's generosity is readily aroused by questions of great religious or artistic interest, it should be added that he displays the utmost parsimony in regard to expenditure on himself or on matters of mere utility. He nevertheless decided, not long ago, to have the electric light in the Vatican, and the benediction was bestowed on the new plant with all due solemnity by Mgr. Pifferi, sacristan of the apostolic palaces, on the 19th February last. The Pope would probably not have made up his mind to the outlay had it not been pointed out to him that there would really be a considerable saving. It was calculated that instead of an annual expenditure of at least £600 on gas, the electric light would not cost more than £72, or a saving of £528 a year, which in three or four years would cover the cost of fitting the electric light. The current was obtained by means of a specially contrived waterfall, forty-three feet in height, the water being supplied from the Eagle basin in the Vatican gardens. The waterfall generates a force equal to ten horse-power, which is transmitted by a turbine to a dynamo, and suffices for the six hundred electric lamps in the Vatican. By order of the Pope, a figure of the Virgin holding the infant Jesus in her arms was placed on one of the walls of the electric lighting shed.

Perhaps, after all, it is a mistake to include the Vatican electric plant among works of mere utility. Doubtless the Pope was not sorry to find an opportunity of once more proving that the Church, though steadfast and immovable in regard to dogma and morals, readily adapts its external existence to the discoveries of modern science, and moves, as the popular expression is, with the times.

CHAPTER III

THE PAPAL FAMILY

Mgr. Angeli—The Pope's confessor—Dr. Lapponi and his patient.

THE Vatican—a prison embellished by its inmate—has often provided material for authors and artists; but the great central figure, Leo XIII, so absorbs the light from the lesser luminaries of his sphere that little is known of them. They include four personages, whose duties bring them into very close intercourse with the Pontiff's august person: his private secretary, Mgr. Angeli; his confessor, Mgr. Pifferi; his medical attendant, Dr. Lapponi; and his valet, Cavaliere Pio Centra (to whom reference will be made in the next chapter).

Mgr. Angeli is about forty years of age. His chief duty is to take charge of his Holiness' private correspondence, but the confidence with which the Pope rightly rewards Mgr. Angeli's exceptional devotion has gradually brought about a considerable increase in this prelate's privileges and prerogatives. Mgr. Angeli is not merely the private secretary of Leo XIII, but his shadow, his confidant, and, if I may use a word which diplomatic etiquette would undoubtedly condemn, his friend. It can be readily understood that the post of secretary to such a man as Leo XIII is not exactly a sinecure. The Pope and

140

his secretary often work sixteen hours a day; and even when
Mgr. Angeli has retired to rest from his labours, it is by no
means certain that his slumbers will not be suddenly dis-
turbed by a summons from the Pope's chamber. Leo XIII
sleeps very little, and as he cannot endure prolonged in-
activity, he frequently fills up the time of waiting for Morpheus
by wooing the Muse, or thinking out some encyclical whereof
the first sheets are lying on his writing-table. Perhaps
his ideas crystallize into some formula which he fears he may
forget before morning. His hand instinctively moves to the
electric button close to his bed. Three minutes later Mgr.
Angeli arrives, half asleep, resignedly seats himself at his
table, and writes, from the Master's dictation, a set of Latin
verses, or one of those wonderful compositions that carry the
bread of truth from Rome to the uttermost parts of the earth.
Mgr. Angeli's friends and all *habitués* of the Vatican constantly wonder how he can endure such a strain, but he does
endure it very well, and has no thought of complaining. His
excessive devotion, it might be said, finds nourishment in the
excessive fatigue to which that devotion condemns him.

The present confessor of Leo XIII is Mgr. Pifferi, an
Augustin friar, who is sacristan of the apostolic palaces.
Like Mgr. Angeli, he is the confidant of the Pope's inmost
thoughts, but after having received them he advises and
orders, his office entitling him to speak with a master's
authority to the head of the Church, when that head of the
Church kneels humbly before him. Every week Leo XIII
implores pardon for his faults like the merest sinner. Every
week, he whose spiritual powers are limited by the Divine

law alone kneels before another man and says, as the humblest
of the faithful would do: "I confess to the Omnipotent
God . . . *and to you, father*, because I have sinned, and I
implore you to intercede for me with Our Lord." And this
man, whom the father of all the faithful calls his father, has
the strange power of invoking Christ's pardon on the Vicar
of Christ: *Ego te absolvo.* What a lesson of humility! To
minds enamoured of liturgical beauties, can the Catholic
religion offer anything more admirable or more touching?

The sacristan or prefect of the apostolic provinces must
always be selected from the order of Augustins. He is *ex-officio*
Bishop of Porphyra, attendant on the throne, prelate of the
Pope's household, adviser to the congregations of Rites, of
Indulgences, and of Relics, member of the Theological College
of the Roman University, member of the Pontifical Committee
on Christian Archæology, and administrator of the pious offerings made to the Madonna del Parto in St. Augustin's. He is
entrusted with the sacred vases, ornaments, and relics in the
Papal chapel, and finally, it is his privilege to administer
extreme unction to the dying Pope. Leo XIII, in spite of his
ninety years, has not yet given Mgr. Pifferi an opportunity
of exercising this privilege. Even during the recent illness,
which caused such deep anxiety in Catholic hearts throughout
the world, the Holy Father's life was at no time in immediate
danger, notwithstanding the pessimistic accounts circulated,
with obviously interested motives, by the adversaries of the
Papacy. Besides, these erroneous reports are often issued in
good faith. The mere arrival of Dr. Lapponi at an unusual
hour, whether he has been sent for or comes of his own

accord, is quite sufficient to give birth to the most sensational stories.

"During my last stay in Rome," the eminent Bishop of Orleans, Mgr. Touchet, told me a few months ago, "it was

Doctor Lapponi.

rumoured that the Pope was dying, and the news of his death was even telegraphed in various directions. The only foundation for the rumour was that the Pope had trapped his finger in a drawer, and that Dr. Lapponi had been sent for to bind up the injured part. On the day after this 'accident' Leo XIII

held the consistory in which the new French bishops were
appointed, and you know how long and tiring the ceremonies
on these occasions are. On the following day (Tuesday) the
Pope presided over a meeting of the Congregation of Rites,
and on the Wednesday he was present at a meeting of the
Cardinals' committee on the Union of the Churches. During
this meeting, which lasted three hours, and at which Cardinal
Langenieux attended, the Pope several times gaily questioned
the venerable Archbishop of Rheims without showing the
slightest trace of suffering. That was not bad for a dying
man, was it? The fact is, that Leo XIII was never better.
I was so struck with his appearance that I ventured to express
the hope that he would become a centenarian.

"'Oh,' he replied, 'only one of my one hundred and sixty-
three predecessors (Gregory IX) ever reached the extreme
limit of old age.'

"' *Unus ne desperes*,' I remarked.

"' *Unus ne confides*,' replied his Holiness, completing the
quotation from St. Augustin.

"It was nevertheless visible that the Pope did not at all
despair of following the example of Gregory IX. My own
impression is, that he may yet live a long time. Some
publishers," Mgr. Touchet added, "have already begun to bring
out books on the next Conclave. These publications irritate
the Pope, who considers them inopportune and in bad taste."

Since this conversation, his Holiness has passed through
a painful crisis, and has had to submit to a surgical operation,
which succeeded perfectly. During this crisis every one at
the Vatican seemed uneasy, except himself. He insisted on

being shown the bulletins signed every morning and
evening by Drs. Mazzoni and Lapponi, and he expressed
surprise at so much alarm having been caused by these
bagatelles! Sometimes he greeted the astonished doctors by
reciting, from memory, a canto of the *Divine Comedy*, or
some poetry he had composed during the night, in spite of
his medical attendants' order that he was not to do any
kind of work. On several occasions he expressed an intention
of composing satires at the expense of those who believed
him to be half dead, and were indulging, rather too early in
the day, in prognostications as to his successor in the Holy
See.

Dr. Lapponi tends his illustrious patient not only with
very great skill but with boundless devotion. This devotion
is all the more meritorious when it is remembered that
Leo XIII is not exactly an easy patient to deal with. Dr.
Lapponi has the utmost trouble to get the Pope to follow
his orders, and often the Pope takes delight in showing
that he can ignore them. For instance, last year, when the
Pope was suffering from hoarseness, Dr. Lapponi prescribed
a powder, and advised his patient to considerably curtail a
discourse he was to deliver during the day. Leo XIII
pocketed the powder and thought no more about it. As
to the discourse, the Holy Father did not omit a word of it.
In vain did the doctor, who was present, repeatedly clear
his throat with much emphasis as a reminder to the Pope
to economize his strength. His Holiness kept on, and even
purposely raised his voice. After finishing his address, he
sent for Dr. Lapponi, handed him the powder, and said,

L

laughing, "Here, my dear doctor, take your powder yourself; you evidently need it more than I."

During the Pope's recent illness, the doctors thought it
their duty to prohibit him from snuff-taking. The illustrious
patient suffered keenly from this deprivation. The times
have greatly changed since Urban VIII and Innocent X
vigorously proscribed tobacco, the former Pope going so far
as to threaten to excommunicate any one who might take
a pinch of snuff within the precincts of the Vatican. The
brief issued on the 1st February, 1659, by Innocent X against
the use of tobacco was abrogated on the 16th January, 1725,
by Benedict XIII, for very good and sufficient reasons. Like
Benedict XIII, Leo XIII takes snuff in large quantities, and
it is well known that Pius IX used to smoke. A snuff-taking
Pope after a smoking Pope! Tobacco is restored to favour
in the Church.

A few years ago Dr. Lapponi narrowly escaped being sup-
planted by Father Kneipp, the Bavarian priest, since deceased,
who prescribed pure water as the sole remedy for all the ills
of poor humanity. This was in 1894. Father Kneipp had been
summoned to Rome by Cardinal Monaco la Valetta, whom he
successfully treated. At this time the Pope experienced pain
in the knee, and complained of intestinal trouble. Cardinal
Monaco la Valetta mentioned Father Kneipp to the Pope, and
the latter agreed to receive the Bavarian priest, who was
reported to have effected some marvellous cures. The Pope
even consented to undress before Father Kneipp, and take a
bath under his superintendence. The news of this caused
considerable stir in the Court and city. The French Ambas-

sador, M. de Béhaine, interviewed the Secretary of State, and
Cardinal Rampolla did not hesitate to respectfully but firmly
reproach the Pope in the name of the Sacred College and the
general interest of the Church. I have no intention of saying
anything derogatory to Father Kneipp and his method, but
although the Pope was only eighty-four years old in 1894,
there was undoubtedly some imprudence in endeavouring to
accustom a man of his age to an entirely new system of hygiene,
and especially one that was in direct opposition to the treatment
he had followed for many years. In any case Father Kneipp
was soon got rid of. He was given the title of prelate instead
of a fee. " I could have made him live to a hundred," said
Father Kneipp when he was told that his services were no
longer required, " but I believe he will live as long as possible,
in spite of the great mistake he has made. His infirmities free
his brain. He is a fortunate man ; he has no body. When
I undressed him for his bath, I first took off his white cassock,
which was stained with snuff, and then sundry skins and
tunics. Beneath these I found little more than a sort of
spectre. Such a man cannot die like others."

Leo XIII has now given his entire confidence to Dr. Lapponi, but he has, I think, still more confidence in himself, his
incredible vitality, and his atavism, for all the Pecci are long-
lived. And then Leo XIII is a trifle—how shall I express
it ?—superstitious. His grandfather died at ninety-six, and
he firmly believes that he will die at the same age. This
confidence, or superstition, as some may call it, does not prevent him from preparing for death every morning, as if the
visitor who will not be denied were sure to knock at his door

before the evening. "Yes," he once said to a French cardinal, "you are right; my health is very good. People say in Rome that every year I live makes me a year younger, and I am almost persuaded to believe it. The Peccis are

Mgr. Constantini, almoner to Leo XIII.

long-lived, but they almost invariably die suddenly, and that is why I always take the precaution of receiving the viaticum at morning mass."

The Pope's secretary, confessor, and physician, the three

The Vatican.—The country house.

functionaries most closely attached to his person, have now been dealt with, and it only remains for us to mention the other members of the Pontifical family in order of rank. They are as follows :—

1. THE CARDINAL PALATINS, so called because they formerly resided in the Pontifical Palace. They are four in number: Cardinal Aloisi Masella, Pro-Datarius, the Pope's deputy in the superintendence of the Datarium ; Cardinal Rampolla, Secretary of State, of whom we shall have occasion to speak in a chapter on the policy of Leo XIII ; Cardinal Macchi, Secretary for Briefs ; and a Cardinal Secretary for Memorials, a post at present vacant.

2. THE PRELATE PALATINS, who also number four : H. E. Mgr. Francis di Sales Della Volpe, his Holiness' majordomo, the future governor of the Conclave, and now superintendent of all the ceremonies in which the Pope and his Court take part; Mgr. Octavius Cagiano di Azevedo, Master of the Chambers, whose jurisdiction extends over everything and everybody connected with the daily working of the Vatican, and to whom all applications for an audience should be addressed ; Mgr. Augustus Guidi, titular Archbishop of Nicæa, auditor to his Holiness, whose chief duty is to examine and report upon all episcopal elections or nominations; and Father Albert Maria Lepidi, Master of the Sacred Apostolic Palace (a post open only to Dominicans), the Pope's theologian (and, in this capacity, censor of all speeches to be delivered before the Holy Father, and of books printed in Rome), and adviser to the Holy Office, the department of Rites, and the Index.

3. Nine ecclesiastical participant secret *camerieri*: Mgr. Joseph Maria Constantini, titular Archbishop of Patras and High Almoner to his Holiness; Mgr. Alexander Volpini, Secretary for Princely Briefs; Mgr. Louis Tripipi, Assistant Secretary of State and Secretary for the Cypher; Mgr. Agapit Panici, Sub-Datarius; Mgr. Vincent Tarozzi, Secretary for Latin Letters; Mgr. Cajetan Bisleti, Cup-bearer; Mgr. Louis Misciatelli, Secretary of Embassy, who conveys the Papal messages to sovereigns and heads of reigning houses; Mgr. Raphael Merry del Val, Master of the Wardrobe; and finally, Mgr. the Prince of Croy, last participant secret *cameriere*, who has no special functions.

4. Mgr. Guglielmo Pifferi, Sacristan of the Apostolic Palaces and Confessor to Leo XIII.

5. Mgr. Cesare Sambucetti, titular Archbishop of Corinth, Secretary to the Congregation of Ceremonials.

6. Prelates of his Holiness' household, comprising : the college of prelates attendant on the throne, the prelatical college of apostolic prothonotaries, the prelatical college of auditors of the Rota, the prelatical college of clerics of the Apostolic Chamber, the prelatical college of voters and referees of the signature, and the college of abbreviators.

7. Secret participant armed *camerieri*.

8. The staff and senior officers of the Noble Guard.

9. Supernumerary ecclesiastical secret *camerieri*.

10. Armed secret *camerieri*.

11. Supernumerary armed *camerieri*.

12. Honorary *camerieri* (in violet).

13. Honorary *camerieri* (*extra urbem*).

14. Honorary armed *camerieri*.
15. Supernumerary honorary *camerieri*.
16. Senior officers of the Swiss Guard.
17. Senior officers of the Palatine Guard.
18. Familiars destined for the religious service.
19. Other familiars.

It will be seen that the cadres of the Papal Court are wide enough to excite and satisfy the legitimate ambition of many. In this respect the Vatican resembles Heaven : " In my Father's house are many mansions."

CHAPTER IV

THE POPE'S DAILY LIFE

Early rising—The Papal toilet—Pio Centra—Mass—Breakfast—
The Vatican goats—Cacciotti and Don Cesare—Audiences—A Protestant at the Vatican—As at the White House—Dinner—The Pope in
his *portentina*—The stables—Returning from a drive—The Pope's
study—In summer quarters—"A bit of France."

LEO XIII rises at six o'clock, or rather his faithful valet,
Cavaliere Pio Centra, enters his room every morning to wake
him (if by chance the Pope should be asleep), and help him
to dress. Usually Pio Centra finds his master risen, or else
the wonderful old man is still at the desk where he had
seated himself the night before, to put the last touch to some
encyclical, or to look over his favourite poets, Dante and
Virgil. The Pope's bed is extremely simple. It is very
narrow, and is raised a step above the marble floor, which is
covered by a thick carpet. In the half-light of the alcove,
festooned by heavy curtains, is an image of the Madonna
sal acro bambino holding the infant Jesus in her arms. At
the foot of the bed, beneath a handsome crucifix, is a *prie-
Dieu*, with the Pope's book of hours resting on a red cushion.
The Papal escutcheon is carved upon this *prie-Dieu*. On it

the Pope offers his first daily prayer, after having devoted a
few moments to a hasty toilet. This toilet, for which the
holy father uses eau de Cologne, is completed later by Pio
Centra, who brushes the Pontiff's hair and shaves him.

The Vatican.—Interior of the country house.

Apropos of this, I am assured that the *valet-de-chambre* of
Pius IX used to distribute the Pontifical bristles among his
friends. That Pio Centra can be persuaded to follow this
example is not so certain, for although Romish fetishism was

not buried, I believe, with Pius IX, it has at least diminished
considerably since the accession of Leo XIII. Besides, the
present Pope's valet, who is a son of a former valet of
Cardinal Pecci, would not be easily corrupted. Some years
ago he owned a hatter's establishment at Rome, which he
gladly handed over to his brother in order to enter the
Pope's service when the post of *ajutante di camera* became
vacant. He has ennobled his humble duties by the devotion
with which they have been fulfilled, and the Pope has shown
his appreciation of this devotion by making him a chevalier
of the Order of Saint Gregory. Pinccio, as Pio Centra is
familiarly called, lives with his family close to the Pope's
private chambers, so that, thanks to the electric bells with
which the palace is now fitted throughout, he can attend to
the smallest requirement of his master.

The Pope generally celebrates mass in a small apartment
adjoining his bedroom, and Pio Centra acts as his acolyte.
The altar is raised only one step. On either side of the
tabernacle, or case in which the pyx is kept, are some
marvellously artistic candelabra and two statues of saints.
On Sundays and fête days, when he is well enough, Leo
XIII celebrates the Holy Sacrament in the chapel leading
into the throne room. This chapel is entirely filled by a
magnificent altar. Those who have obtained the much-
desired privilege of attending the celebration remain in the
adjoining room, the door of which is kept open, and are
afterwards presented to the Holy Father, who gives them his
blessing with a few kind words. Leo XIII says mass very
slowly, with deep reverence, and a full consciousness of the

grandeur of this service, which may well, as the Church
teaches, inspire awe in the angels themselves. It is within
the power of the lowliest of priests to transform the consecrated elements into the Divine substance, but when the
celebrant is the Vicar of Christ, when the Pope, with face
divinely illuminated and with trembling hands, bends over
the immaculate host or golden chalice, is there not in this
always sublime act something still more sublime?

After having celebrated the holy sacrifice, the Pope
attends another mass, said by the chaplain on duty. This
is his thanksgiving. He then breakfasts on a little chocolate
or *café au lait*. Since 1888, the sacerdotal jubilee of Leo
XIII, the milk has been supplied by goats penned within
the myrtle hedges of the Vatican gardens, near the Zitella
fountain. Rustic and simple as in the days of his youth, the
Carpinetans, who wished to present him with a jubilee
offering, sent their compatriot a flock of goats, under the
escort of a shepherd named Cacciotti. The Pope often visits
this flock, caresses the gentle animals, and converses with the
shepherd from his native place. Cardinal Rampolla arrives
about eight o'clock, and is immediately conducted into the
presence of the Holy Father. After this daily interview
granted to the eminent Secretary of State, the Pope, if the
weather be fine, takes a short walk in the Vatican gardens.
He does not disdain to occasionally chat with the gardener,
and even give him good advice, for the Pope is by no means
ignorant of horticulture, and is keenly interested in agri-
culture, as Don Cesare, the gardener, learnt one day to his
cost. On that occasion the Pope summoned Don Cesare and

complained about some ivy which appeared to be in a pitiable condition.

"Why are you letting this plant die?" the Pope asked.

"Holy Father, the soil is so bad."

"You don't know what you are talking about, or else you think we believe everything you may please to tell us."

Then followed a regular lecture which made the mortified Don Cesare exclaim, when the Pope had disappeared—

"He can teach every one, from the cardinals to his gardener. You can't get over him."

After his walk come the receptions. One by one he receives those dignitaries who have regular stated audiences several times a week with his Holiness to dispose of current business, either connected with the internal administration of the Vatican, or the general government of the Church. These audiences include the prefect of the apostolic palaces, the major-domo, the prefects of the various congregations, etc., and visitors who have been granted a private audience. For these audiences there is a special ceremonial; first, the threefold salutation, one at the entrance door, a second in the centre of the apartment, the third when kissing the Pope's slipper. The Pope does not rise, and the visitor remains standing throughout the audience. It rests with the Holy Father to say when it shall be finished. The visitor must step backward when retiring, so as to avoid turning his back upon the head of the Church. This ceremonial applies to Roman Catholics only. It is a curious fact, that the Papal masters of ceremonies have never drawn up any code of etiquette applying to receptions of non-

Roman Catholics, although these have been fairly frequent during the reign of Leo XIII. When a distinguished American Protestant, to whom the Pope had granted a private audience, asked the major-domo what ceremonial he was to observe, the official was obliged to refer to the Pope for instructions. "Tell him," commanded his Holiness, "to do just as if he were being received by the President of the United States."

The Pope dines at two o'clock. I have already spoken of his extreme abstemiousness. He takes a *consommé*, some eggs, rarely any meat, Bordeaux wine (supplied gratis for some years past by a women's community in the Gironde), and nothing more. Dare I mention the fact, however, that Leo XIII is extremely fond of salad, mixed with plenty of vinegar? Alas! salad is forbidden his Holiness by Dr. Lapponi, but it happens sometimes that the Pope evades all supervision. A few months ago Leo XIII was taken ill in the middle of the night, and humbly confessed to the hastily summoned doctor a disobedience which it was impossible to hide from him.

The Pope always dines alone. Formerly dinners used to be regularly provided at the Vatican at two o'clock for twelve guests of distinction, but they dined after the Pope had finished. For some reason this custom is no longer kept up. Sometimes Leo XIII pays his secretary the compliment of inviting him to his table. Mgr. Angeli sits down to the meal, and converses freely with the Pontiff, but eats nothing. However, the Pope attaches little importance to such matters, and he despatches his meals with a rapidity which

is the despair of the good Dr. Lapponi and the head
cook.

After his dinner the Pope takes a short nap followed by
a drive. The *sediarii* carry him in a special chair called the
portentina, as far as the garden railings or the Paul V gate,
where he is awaited either by a black landau with red wheels,
and lined inside with white damask, or a large varnished
wood vehicle, also upholstered in white damask. The Pope
gives the preference to this latter conveyance. Pius IX used
it often during his country visits to Castel Gandolfo. The
other carriage is a comparatively recent acquisition. Both
are drawn by a pair of large black Roman horses. The
Vatican stables can boast of only twelve horses (four of
which are used by the Noble Guards, and four by the
Pontifical Court) and two mules, which are harnessed to the
conveyances especially reserved for transporting ecclesiastical
objects sent by the Pope to the Roman churches. When
Leo XIII has taken his place in the *portentina*, the
Pontifical procession is formed. It consists of two Swiss
Guards carrying halberds, and two Noble Guards preceding
the chair-bearers, after whom come an officer of the Noble
Guard and a chamberlain. The procession generally crosses
the Raphael rooms, map galleries, tapestry and candelabra
salons, and reaches the garden by the grand staircase of the
museum, where the Pope, before getting into his carriage,
throws a red mantle over his shoulders, and puts on a hat
of the same colour. The carriage, with its two footmen
standing behind in black coats and high hats to match the
coachman, is escorted by mounted Noble Guards. Any

person accompanying the Pope sits opposite, not beside him.
The drive, which usually lasts two hours, is always taken in
the same place, through a magnificent avenue of plane trees
and oaks, extending from the Angelica Gate to the Caval-
leggeri Gate.   Whilst driving the Holy Father reads, or talks
to those who accompany him.   Sometimes he gets out of the
carriage and walks for a few moments with the help of a
gold-headed cane.   To be sure, he can manage without this
cane, and he displays a certain amount of pride in so doing,
and even walking more briskly when there are rumours in
Rome that the Pope is ill.

M. Ch. Formentin, who was once fortunate enough to be
present when the Pope was re-entering his apartments, has
written the following curious and charming sketch of what he
saw :—"The chair was gently deposited by the *sediarii* on the
marble floor ; the door opened, and the Pope appeared.   His
wasted body, bent forward in the act of leaving the chair,
sprang erect as if impelled by springs of steel.   There was
an air of majesty about the tall, willowy form, and the head,
a splendid one, was fascinating.   The features were fleshless.
There seemed to be hardly a drop of blood beneath the dried
and withered skin.   The broad forehead was pale as ivory,
and the lips were colourless, but the eyes lit up and vivified
this living skeleton.   I shall never forget those eyes.   The
fire that issued from them seemed to have consumed the face
in which they were set.   They were black, deeply-set and
piercing.   They seemed to probe the inmost depths of one's
soul.   There was something terrifying in their brilliancy.

"The Pope came towards us with an airy lightness in

M

his tread. Earthly clay appeared to have no part in the frail white form gliding before us like a great wing. His hand, which might have been a spectre's, so diaphanous was it, waved gentle benedictions on our bowed heads. The Pope

The throne room in the Vatican.

stopped for a moment. He had noticed a priest—a Jesuit— to whom he deigned to address a few words. His voice was not a far-off echo, but clear, resonant, and slightly nasal. A few steps more and Leo XIII reached his apartments; the

apparition vanished behind a red velvet door, and we heard
the sharp, repeated calls of an electric bell. It was the Pope,
at work again, summoning his secretary."

The Pope's study is of the simplest possible kind. It con-

The round room in the Leonine tower.

tains an official desk with a crucifix above it, and a few chairs
upholstered in red stuff. Opposite, and at some distance
from the desk, are an arm-chair and a tiny table covered with
green velvet. Behind the hangings is a cage of little birds,

which enliven the austere surroundings by their joyous
twittering.

During the summer the Pontiff spends nearly the whole
of the day in the historic Leonine tower. This massive
structure dates from the end of the ninth century and the
reign of Leo IV, who built it to protect the city of Rome
against the Saracens. It formed part of the fortifications,
which extended from the Castle of St. Angelo, up the
Vatican hill, skirted the Tiber, and joined the Aurelian wall.
The Leonine tower consists of three floors. The Pope usually
occupies a large round room lighted by two windows. The
walls are nearly sixteen feet thick. In the recess of a
third window, walled up, is a couch on which the Holy
Father can enjoy the siesta so dear to the Roman heart. I
should also mention an exact reproduction of the Massabiella
grotto in the most poetical and charming spot in the palace.
A statue of our Lady of Lourdes stands in the hollow of the
rock. The Sovereign Pontiff often has himself carried to
this grotto to tell his beads. He delights in tending the
flowers growing all around. When a cardinal asked him one
day why he visited this spot so frequently, Leo XIII replied,
"It's my bit of France."

The Pope sups at ten o'clock, after having told his rosary,
in company with the prelates on duty, in his private chapel.
Then he has newspapers read to him, the passages most
likely to interest him having been previously marked and
annotated by the Secretary of State, and by Mgr. Angeli. He
is still at work when all others within the palace are at rest,
and his lamp is never extinguished before midnight, or one
o'clock in the morning.

CHAPTER V

A POLITICAL POPE

Leo XIII and political cemeteries—*From Toast to Encyclical*—A precedent—Pius VI and the Directory—Influence of the Papal policy on St. Peter's Pence—Opposition to the Pontifical directions—The Pope's firmness and justice—Cardinal Rampolla—M. Lefebvre de Behaine—M. Poubelle—Leo XIII and Bismarck.

I AM acquainted with certain Pharisees—the species has perpetuated itself since the days of the Evangelists—who are scandalized if they hear such a thing as "the Pope's policy" alluded to. As if the most important religious questions, such as liberty to teach, the exemption of clerics from military service, marriage, and many other subjects, were not closely connected with civil legislation and consequently with politicals, such legislation being the work of a political assembly; as if the temporal end of political society were not dependent upon the spiritual end of religious society; as if it were not a binding obligation on the Pope, whose subjects are to be found in every kingdom, empire, and republic in the world, to endeavour to maintain good relations with the various governments, so that they will not only respect but enforce respect for the religious interests of these subjects! Political influence is the most powerful of human agencies;

165

it may be said to be the crystallization of all the human
agencies that God desires the Pope to use for the government
of the Church, because, the Church being a society composed
of human beings, it must be governed by human means. Leo
XIII has realized this truth better than perhaps any of his
predecessors. History will record, to his eternal honour, that
he was, in the highest and purest acceptation of the word, a
political Pope.

At the accession of Leo XIII the Holy See was on bad
terms with most governments, and a most dangerous misunderstanding existed between the Church and the people.
To remove this misunderstanding, and to reconcile the
Papacy with the governments was the twofold task to which
the new Pope applied himself—a colossal enterprise requiring
the utmost efforts of his genius.

"Think," writes M. de Vogüé, "of the amount of decision
required from him; think of the enormous pressure brought
to bear on him by his ordinary *clientèle* with a view to
maintaining him in what had seemed to him to be his
destined *rôle* as head of the Church: the chaplain of a
cemetery, instructed to keep a pious watch over the political
tombs in the shelter of the sanctuary. At the age of eighty
Leo XIII issued from this cemetery, and threw himself into
the world of the living, to fight for its possession against
adversaries who thought themselves its unquestioned masters.
He hearkened unto the words of the Saviour: "Leave the
dead to bury their dead." To him might be applied the
words of Sir Francis Drake: "From the mountain height he
saw the new ocean, and launched a fisher's bark upon it."

But although Leo XIII's government of the Church differs from that of Pius IX, it would not be just to institute a comparison to the disadvantage of the late Pope. There are certainly differences, but there is no contradiction between the words and acts of the "Syllabus Pope" and those of the Pontiff who issued the encyclical of the 16th February, 1892, to the French Catholics, and the *Rerum novarum* encyclical. This truth has never been brought out in stronger relief than by the Abbé Bertrin, the eminent author of *Grandes Figures Catholiques*. He writes:—"The Pope who spoke of 'necessary affirmations' has been succeeded, under God, by the Pope who favours 'opportune conciliation.' With the object of proclaiming the truths needed by the world, the one excited universal anger against the Church; the other has been engaged in signing treaties of peace. Without abandoning one iota of the doctrines which he holds as a sacred inheritance from his predecessor, he is allaying mistrust and the unfriendliness arising from it. He appears to be occupied with something quite different from the work of Pius IX, but in reality he is continuing and completing it."

The Pontifical policy in France may be summed up in one short formula : the obligation of all Catholics to unreservedly support the Republic. The evolution of this policy, and the contradictory manifestations it has excited in France, are set forth with the utmost clearness in the very interesting and informing work published by M. Georges Goyau, the distinguished writer on the staff of the *Revue des Deux Mondes*, under the title, *From Toast to Encyclical*. As the reader will have guessed, the "toast" was the remarkable speech delivered by Cardinal Lavigerie on the 12th November, 1890, to the officers of the French squadron, who were received by the illustrious Primate of Africa, in the absence of the Governor-General of Algeria.

"In view of our still bleeding past," said the Cardinal, "and of our ever-threatening future, union is our great need. Union is also, let me tell you, the foremost wish of the Church and of all its pastors of every degree. The Church does not ask us to either give up the remembrance of past glories or the sentiments of fidelity and gratitude that are an honour to every man. But when the will of a people has been definitely expressed, when the form of government, as Leo XIII recently stated, is in no way contrary to the principles on which alone civilized and Christian nations can exist, when the unreserved acceptance of this form of government is necessary to preserve a people from danger, the time has come to declare the ordeal over, to end our dissensions, and to sacrifice all that conscience and honour allow us to sacrifice for the safety of our country. Without this patriotic acceptance of the situation nothing can avail either to maintain peace and order, to save the world from the social danger, or to preserve even the religion of which we are the ministers. It would be folly to attempt to support the columns of an edifice without going inside it, if only to prevent those who would destroy everything from accomplishing their mad design. It would be still greater folly to attack the building from without, as some are even now doing, in spite of recent scandals : disclosing our ambitions and hatreds to observant enemies, and instilling into the heart of France the discouragement that precedes the final catastrophe."

The encyclical of the 16th February, 1892, addressed to

Mgr. Pifferi, sacristan to Leo XIII.

the French Catholics, was the corollary of Cardinal Lavigerie's speech, which was directly inspired by Leo XIII. In this encyclical the Pope thus expressed himself:—

"When the new governments that represent this im-

mutable power are constituted, recognition of them is not
only permissible but required, and even necessitated, by the
demands of the social welfare by which they are created and
maintained." *

Thus Rome spoke. The hearing was over, and judgment
given. The immense majority of bishops, priests, and laymen
submitted, in spite of an attempted revival of Gallicanism by
certain organs of those political cemeteries the chaplaincy of
which Leo XIII had so decidedly refused.

It cannot be too strongly pointed out, that the doctrine
contained in the encyclical is by no means new to the
Church. Jesus Christ taught it when He said to His dis-
ciples, "Render unto Cæsar the things that are Cæsar's."
St. Paul taught it when he wrote, "Servants, obey your
masters." In modern times, a century before Leo XIII
urged French Catholics to accept the Republic, Pius VI advised the French Catholics of his day to accept the Directory.
The most essential part of the Papal utterance is as follows :—

"We should fail in our duty if we did not eagerly seize
upon all opportunities to exhort you to peace, and to cause
you to realize the necessity of submission to the constituted
authorities. It is a recognized dogma of the Catholic religion,
that governments are established by divine wisdom to avoid
anarchy and confusion, and to prevent peoples from being
tossed hither and thither like the waves of the sea. Thus
St. Paul, speaking not of one special prince, but of the
principle itself, affirms that there is no power not proceeding
from God, and that to resist this power is to resist the decrees
of God Himself. Thus, our dear sons, do not be led away, do

not allow an ill-directed piety to furnish the adherents of the
new order with occasion to deny the Catholic religion. Your
disobedience would be a crime involving severe punishment,
not only by the powers of this earth, but, which is far worse,
by God Himself, who threatens eternal damnation to those
who attempt to withstand Him. Thus, our dear sons, we
exhort you, in the name of our Lord Jesus Christ, to set
yourselves with all your hearts and minds to prove your submission to those who are set over you. In so doing you will
render unto God the obedience which is His due, and you
will prove to your governors that the true religion is in no
way designed to upset civil law. Your conduct will convince
them more and more every day of this truth, and will induce
them to cherish and protect your religion by favouring the
observance of the precepts of the Gospel and the rules of
ecclesiastical discipline. Finally, we warn you to give no
heed to any one who may put forward a doctrine other than
this as the true doctrine of the Apostolic See. And we give
you our Apostolic benediction with paternal tenderness.
Given in Rome, at Santa Maria Maggiore, under the Fisherman's ring, this 5th day of July, 1796, the 22nd year of our
Pontificate. Signed: R. Card. Braschius de Honestis."

Thus there is nothing new in the position of the Church,
which, as Leo XIII one day expressed it to Monsieur de
Blowitz, "holds fast to a single body, which is itself held fast
upon the cross!"

Nevertheless, though the doctrine contained in the 1892
encyclical was not new, its application to the present Government of France constituted an innovation, and even a very

daring innovation, if we bear in mind the political position
taken up by the clergy, who were closely united by important
interests to the dispossessed parties. There was quite a
revolution in Catholic minds and habits. The few priests
who had already declared themselves Republicans were at
first looked upon with suspicion, and their churches were
shunned by the devout. Directly after the encyclical, the
priests who continued to call themselves Monarchists—a still
smaller number—saw the wise among the clergy turn away
from them. The very devout were slower in comprehending
the change, and it actually happened that in more than one
religious coterie prayers were offered for the conversion of the
Pope !

The rich Monarchist laymen who were accustomed to
subscribe liberally to all the principal Catholic works weakly
showed their discontent by cutting down their offerings to
Peter's Pence ; and more than one prelate took upon himself
to convey the grievances of his dissatisfied flock to the
Vatican. The bishop of a diocese quite near to Paris ventured to say to the Pope :—

" Holy Father, may I speak frankly ? "

" Certainly."

" Well, your Holiness is being deceived. The situation in
France is not what you believe it to be. Your intervention
in the politics of that country has produced quite a feeling of
disaffection for your person. This is proved by the fact that
the subscription to Peter's Pence, which amounted to £60,000
last year in my diocese, has now fallen to £35,200. If you
will allow me, I will repeat a remark made to me by an

excellent Catholic in my diocese, who said, 'I cannot love the Pope now that he has become a republican.'"

The Pope merely replied by the smile of a man who had foreseen this kind of opposition, and who did not attach too much importance to it. A few days afterwards, when giving audience to the *curé* of one of the most important parishes in Paris, he said, "I wish to commit the Church so fully that it will be impossible for my successor to turn back."

Opposition to the Pope's policy was not by any means confined to the French Catholics. It displayed itself even in the *entourage* of the Holy Father, on various occasions and in various forms. The manner in which Leo XIII met this opposition, and his conduct towards his opponents, throw a strong light on the unshakable firmness of his character, as well as on his sense of justice. Two anecdotes may be cited in illustration of this. One of the earliest opponents among those most closely approaching the Pope was Cardinal Parocchi, his Holiness' Vicar. This prelate's opposition was so clearly displayed on one occasion that Leo XIII asked him in unmistakable terms to resign.

"What your Holiness asks of me is very serious," replied the Cardinal. "I beg your Holiness to grant me a few days for reflection."

Two days afterwards Leo XIII sent for Cardinal Parocchi. "Well, Cardinal, have you decided?" he asked.

"Not yet. Will your Holiness kindly wait another two days?"

At the end of that period Cardinal Parocchi was again admitted to the presence of Leo XIII. "Holy Father," he said, "I have fully reflected, and I consider it my duty to remain at my post so long as your Holiness does not think fit to relieve me of it."

In the meantime Leo XIII had also reflected; and he came to the conclusion that a political difference of opinion could not justify him in punishing Cardinal Parocchi, whose theological and philosophical knowledge, eminent administrative qualities, and distinguished virtues he fully appreciated and admired.

The other anecdote relates to Cardinal Oreglia, the *doyen* of the Sacred College. Cardinal Oreglia, whose great personal worth and high standing in the Church entitle him to speak freely to the Pope himself, once abused the privilege to such an extent as to draw down upon himself this undisguised threat :—

"Will your Eminence please remember that I can not only bestow the hat but take it away?"

"Holy Father," quietly replied Cardinal Oreglia, "you have that power, but if you use it against me, I shall consider myself happy to suffer for having spoken the truth."

This incident occurred at the beginning of the year 1884. On the 27th March following, Leo XIII, realizing that in Cardinal Oreglia he had to deal with a man and not with a courtier, appointed him camerlengo of the Holy Roman Church, or, as we have already explained, the eventual head of the executive power during the next vacancy in the Holy See.

We now come to Cardinal Rampolla, Secretary of State to the Holy See, who is one of the most disinterested and

firm supporters of the Pope's policy, especially in regard to
France. I say the most disinterested, because in espousing
all the Holy Father's ideas, and sacrificing his own personality
until he appeared to be nothing more than the Pope's
political shadow, Cardinal Rampolla well knew that he was
destroying all his chance of succeeding Leo XIII. I also
say the most devoted, because Cardinal Rampolla has truly
and constantly striven to carry out the Pope's orders with
the most complete forgetfulness of self. During the last
ten years he has left Rome only once, and that was to be
present at his sister's death-bed. Cardinal Rampolla is,
besides, the acutest, the most discreet, and the best-informed
of diplomatists. As one who knew him wrote:—"How
pleasant and charming he manages to be at all the audiences
he gives every day, and how the visitor is led to say all he
knows and gets nothing in return, but nevertheless goes
away delighted!"

It would be unjust not to pay homage in this work to
the memory of Count Lefebvre de Béhaine, who was French
Ambassador to the Holy See for thirteen years, and supported
the Holy Father's French policy with all his intelligence
and all his power. As M. Francis Charmes wrote on the
day after the death of M. de Béhaine:—"The Holy Father's
intellect and personality are sufficiently marked to discourage
any attempt to exaggerate the influence our Ambassador
may have had over him; but it is not too much to say that
M. Lefebvre de Béhaine facilitated all that has been done.
If we may judge of the merits of a diplomatist by the
relations he has established or strengthened between the

Government he represents and the one to which he is accredited, it must be admitted that the services of M. Lefebvre de Béhaine have been far above the common,

Mace-bearer and chaplain to Leo XIII.

especially when it is remembered that he represented the French Republic at a time when it was still distracted by political conflicts, in which religious intercourse with the

The Vatican.—The country house.

highest and most imperial—if we may be allowed to use a word now applied to so many things—spiritual power had been clumsily confused and endangered. If we examine the state of our relations with the Holy See at the commencement of M. de Béhaine's mission, and if we compare it with what those relations were at the end, we can estimate the progress accomplished; and whatever may be attributable to the spontaneous initiative of the Holy Father, our Ambassador certainly had his own share."

The Radical party, on coming into office in the autumn of 1895, discovered that this good servant ought to be recalled. "Of all the mistakes committed by the Radicals" (to again quote M. Francis Charmes), "this one was the most logical on their part." Nothing could be truer, but it is hardly likely that the Radicals will find any cause for vanity in such logic. War with the Church has always been the spring-board of Radicalism. The object steadily pursued by M. Lefebvre de Béhaine was a *rapprochement* between France and the Holy See, and that being so, he was bound to be sacrificed, but what his "workman's hand," to use the expression in favour during the *grand siècle*, had accomplished, still endured.

The successor of this excellent "workman" was an apprentice—in the diplomatic sense—in the person of M. Poubelle, who knew nothing of Rome, of the Pope, of Roman society, or of the Pontifical policy. The new Ambassador was soon estimated at his true value, which was not considered great. His failure was complete. And yet the ex-Prefect of the Seine did all in his power to become a *persona grata*

at the Vatican. Having heard that the Pope sometimes
forgot himself to the extent of perpetrating Latin verses,
and that he was by no means destitute of the author's
amour-propre, it occurred to M. Poubelle to learn some of
these verses, and pay the Pope the delicate flattery of reciting
them on the first opportunity. The Ambassador, however,
mistrusted his memory. When the eventful day arrived, he
thought it wise to put a manuscript copy of the verses inside
his hat, so that he could refer to it for assistance in playing
his part. The fraud was even more clumsy than the flattery
was opportune, and the chance of the Pope being taken in
by it was still further reduced by the happy-go-lucky way
in which M. Poubelle recited the Pope's charming lines.
The Pontiff's keen, ironical glance no sooner met his eye
than he stopped short, like a school-boy caught in the act of
committing some misdemeanour. The story soon became
known, and excited much sarcasm at the diplomatist's
expense. M. Poubelle has lately been succeeded by M.
Nisard, and it can only be hoped that the latter will realize
the hopes aroused by his appointment.

Hitherto I have dealt only with the Pope's policy in
regard to France, but it is known that Leo XIII has been
guided by the same lofty and conciliatory motives in his
relations with all foreign governments, and that success, to a
greater or less extent, has always attended the generous
inspirations of his great mind. Many interesting anecdotes
are connected with his dealings with Germany, which ended
in the abrogation of the Kulturkampf. Some very curious
revelations on the religious policy of Prince Bismarck and

the relations between the Iron Chancellor and Leo XIII, have been made by Geffcken, the confidant and executor of Frederick II and the implacable enemy of Bismarck, who caused him to be tried in 1888 by the High Court at Leipzig, and sentenced to exile for publishing some of the late Emperor's private papers in the *Deutsche Rundschau*, this publication being treated as a " criminal disclosure of State secrets." Geffcken paid his first visit to Rome in 1876, that being his first diplomatic journey *ad limina*, but on that occasion he merely had an unimportant conversation with Cardinal Antonelli. He was sent a second time, in March 1882, by Marshal von Manteuffel, with definite instructions to request the Sovereign Pontiff to forbid the Alsatian clergy from taking part in the anti-German agitation. Geffcken was then State Councillor for Alsace-Lorraine. Cardinal Jacobini, with whom he had a preliminary interview, would bind himself to nothing, and advised him to see the Pope. Geffcken immediately asked for an audience, and it was granted for the following Sunday. It was, however, adjourned till next day. The Grand Duke Alexis had arrived in Rome and had asked for an audience, which the Pope fixed for the same day, thus openly giving the Tsar's envoy the preference over the representative of the German Government. This fact is worthy of attention, because it marks a period in the policy of friendliness to Russia to which the Holy Father, henceforth desirous for the Franco-Russian alliance, afterwards adhered so faithfully. When Geffcken obtained his audience, he laid the complaints of the German Government before the Holy Father, but he himself admits that he did not obtain a definite answer.

" I authorize you," said Leo XIII, "to assure the Marshal that I will see to it."

This reply did not commit the Pope to much, and, as a matter of fact, the Nuncio at Munich never received any instructions in reference to the mission which had formed the object of Geffcken's second journey to Rome. The German diplomatist complains in bitter terms of this failure to give him any satisfaction.

Nevertheless the Pope, though inflexible in matters of principle, thought it his duty to make the German Government a concession of another kind. M. Winterer, the leader of the anti-German association, was to have been raised to the dignity of an apostolic prothonotary. His appointment did not take place, but the general situation of Germany from the religous point of view was not altered by the sacrifice of M. Winterer. The conflict excited by the rigorous application of the Acts passed in May 1876, was carried on with greater fury than ever, and imperilled not only the interests of Catholicism but of German predominance. The Chancellor continued his negotiations with the Holy See, not only ceding nothing, but requiring from the Pope a sacrifice of his principles, to which it was impossible for his Holiness to consent. The *desiderata* of Leo XIII were nevertheless—as Geffcken, a Protestant, admits—extremely moderate. What he desired was not even a concordat, but merely a revision of German ecclesiastical legislation by means of a Government measure, which should bind both parties by reciprocal concessions, and do away with such provisions of the Falk laws as were intolerable to Catholics. Bismarck's only reply to these very

legitimate demands was to stop more and more ecclesiastical
stipends, and drive the *élite* of the clergy into exile. Bismarck
(who had, according to Count Beust, when at Versailles in

Mgr. Della Volpe, major-domo to Leo XIII.

1871, made the Sovereign Pontiff an offer to transfer the
Holy See to Cologne) flattered himself that this odious
persecution would overcome the resistance offered by the
Roman Court to his hitherto all-powerful will. But neither

the Pope nor the German Catholics, represented by the Centre under the leadership of the valiant Windthorst, yielded an inch of ground. As Geffcken remarks, " the Church could wait, but the Chancellor became more and more anxious for the end." Eventually, in 1884, Bismarck, who had solemnly declared four years before that any revision of the May laws was impossible, was obliged to seriously consider that revision. He took refuge in an assertion that "other hands" had spoiled the great plan conceived by him; but, as Geffcken observes, that was Bismarck's usual excuse when events disappointed his hopes and upset his profound combinations. Geffcken facetiously urges the ex-Chancellor to do homage to truth, and reveal to the world whose were those "other hands."

Matters were in this position when the extraordinary Caroline Islands affair cropped up. Geffcken gives a very curious account of the circumstances which induced Bismarck to submit his difference with Spain over these islands to the arbitration of the Holy Father. "In the brain of this Machiavelian pachyderm, who could neither advance nor retreat," writes M. de Blowitz, "there originated an archaic idea which excited universal surprise. With elephantine irony, Prince von Bismarck offered Leo XIII the post of arbitrator between Spain and Germany." According to Geffcken, M. de Blowitz and the Press of the entire world were mistaken. The idea of Papal arbitration did not originate with the "pachyderm" Bismarck. It was suggested to him, and he fell into a clumsily laid trap. He had occupied the Caroline Islands, which were worth very little, and had already been given up by the Spanish Government,

when the aspect of affairs was suddenly altered by a riot at
Madrid. A mob broke into the German Legation. The
German Minister was insulted. The Spanish Government was
obliged, under the pressure of public opinion, to reaffirm its
alleged rights, and to claim the privileges of Spain as the
first occupant of the islands. Matters, however, had already
gone too far to allow Prince Bismarck to give way without
injury to the dignity of the Empire, and he immediately
ordered the publication of two documents establishing the
rights of Germany; but a despatch from the Emperor soon
upset the Chancellor's plans. This despatch stated that the
Spanish Monarchy must not be endangered, and that the
young King, having to some extent thrown himself, during
his recent visit to Germany (September 1883), on the
generosity of the Emperor, it would be unseemly for the
German Government to act harshly towards him. The
position was very difficult for Bismarck. As M. de Blowitz
well says, the Prince could neither advance nor retreat. At
this stage an Italian journalist, whom Bismarck had expelled
from Germany, conceived a colossal practical joke. He sent
a telegram to a Berlin newspaper, announcing that the
Spanish Government was about to ask the Pope to intervene.
Bismarck took this story *au sérieux* and intercepted the
telegram. Then, believing that he was about to accomplish
a diplomatic master-stroke, he resolved to be beforehand with
Spain, and propose the arbitration of which not a single
Spanish statesman had thought for a moment. Although the
Pope's decision was in favour of Spain, it brought about quite
a *détente* between Berlin and Rome. The Pope sent the

Chancellor the Order of Christ, with an autograph letter in
which he said the strength of Germany depended on the
co-operation of the Catholic Church. The Chancellor wrote
to the Pope, asking him to order the Centre to support the
Government, and offering him certain concessions in return.
As is known, the Centre remained deaf to all exhortations,
and refused to give up one iota of the Catholic claims or a
single line of its political programme. It does not, moreover,
appear that the Pope disapproved of this attribute, inasmuch
as, in an address to the German pilgrims on the 21st April,
1885, he congratulated them on the "good appearance" preserved by Catholics in their country. In any case, it is certain
that the Papal diplomacy very largely contributed to the abolition of the Kulturkampf.

The reign of Leo XIII has also witnessed the official
re-establishment of relations between Russia and the Holy
See. In Great Britain the Pope's letter to the English led
to numerous conversions. In America the Pope has exerted
all his influence in favour of the religious revival, but at the
same time he has striven to confine the imprudent zeal of the
innovators within the bounds of orthodoxy. In every part
of the world he has pursued the great work of the union of
the Churches through a return to Catholic unity. He has
shown himself intransigent in regard to one Government
only, the Italian, because any compromise on his part with
the Government which confiscated the temporal power of
the Popes, and thereby affected the independence of the Holy
See, would have been equivalent to an abandonment of the
imprescriptible rights of the Church.

CHAPTER VI

THE POPE AND THE PRESS

The first interviewer—Brethren at enmity—Special correspondents at the Vatican—A French woman journalist and the Pope—What Leo XIII thinks of Anti-Semitism.

"*Si facciamo uno periodico !*" (Suppose we start a paper.) This remark was made, not without a shade of irony, by Cardinal Franchi to Leo XIII, who had just been expatiating on the utility of the head of the Church publicly expressing his opinion, on the great public questions of the day. The Pope has not yet started a paper, but he justly attributes importance to the Press. He would wish to use it as a lever with which, like another Archimedes, to move the world, and he generally receives journalists with marked favour. The first to whom he gave audience at the Vatican was Louis Veuillot. The new Pope spoke of the immense services that could be rendered to the Catholic religion by journalists who were both earnest Catholics and men of talent.

"Do you know many of that description?" added the Pope with a smile. "And will you be able to leave the *Univers* in good hands when you are no longer there to edit it ? "

187

Louis Veuillot mentioned two names, those of MM. Loth and Auguste Roussel. Alas! what remains of Louis Veuillot's work to-day? The *Univers* still survives, and fights the good fight against the adversaries of the Papal directions, but it has not escaped those internal divisions to which the words of Christ may be applied—" Every kingdom divided against itself is brought to desolation." MM. Loth and Auguste Roussel, the two spiritual children of the great controversialist, are just those who have brought about the schism. The outcome was the *Vérité*, and that paper had hardly come into existence before it engaged in a deadly struggle, yet undecided, with the *Univers*. It need hardly be said that this conflict is a distress to Catholics, who would prefer to see these two brethren unite their forces against the common enemy.

The most remarkable feature of this fratricidal struggle is the fact, perhaps unprecedented, that the Pope took part in it by administering a public and official reprimand to one of the contending newspapers, through the Secretary of State. The *Vérité* not having since mended its ways, it has obtained none of the benedictions for which the religious papers are accustomed to implore the Holy Father at stated intervals. The staff of the *Vérité* are consequently left with the unpleasant alternative of either committing professional suicide, or discounting the accession of a Pope who will be less severe towards the line of conduct which is their *raison d'être*.

I have stated that Leo XIII takes a great interest in the Press, and the example I have just cited is a sufficiently good proof of the assertion. I added that the Pope usually receives

journalists with marked favour. This is shown by the fact that
he has not disdained to allow himself to be interviewed on
several occasions. I think I may say without fear of contradiction, that he is the first Pope who ever took this means of
placing himself in touch with public opinion. It is true that
the interview is a comparatively recent journalistic method,
but it is none the less curious to see the head of the Church
"sitting," if I may use the expression, to a reporter just
as he afterwards sat to the painter Chartran, and, as a climax
of modernism, to a biograph. M. Charles Benoist was right
when he wrote that " on the symbolic stone, by a combination
of the very old and the very new, Leo XIII has built a bell-
tower and discovered a style."

The journalists whom the Pope has allowed to interview
him are of course not very numerous. I have already referred
to M. de Blowitz, and I should mention the interview with
Leo XIII which appeared in the *Petit Journal* on the 17th
February, 1892, under the signature of M. Judet. This
interview created a great sensation in consequence of the
Pope's important statement:—"I am of opinion that all
citizens should remain within the limits of the law. Every
one may maintain his own private preferences, but when
action is concerned, there can only be the government that
France has chosen." M. Louis Joubert, writing on this
subject in the *Correspondant*, says:—"In the time of the
Apostles, as in the days of the Crusades, the Church appealed
to the multitude. Leo XIII desires to have his ideas
conveyed, by means appropriate to the new conditions of
society, and undistorted by prejudice and calumny, to the

remotest village of our country. This is why the most
widely read of French newspapers, the *Petit Journal,* was
given the honour of disseminating the Pope's words and
bringing them into the dwellings of even those who have

Mgr. Sambucetti and Count Soderini, Masters of the
Ceremonies to Leo XIII.

never crossed the threshold of their *curé.*" Quite recently
M. Boyer d'Agen ventured to question the Pope on the
Dreyfus case, and brought back from Rome a grand declaration
of justice and charity.

Of all the interviews to which Leo XIII has consented, the most curious and remarkable is the one given to Mme. Séverine (the well-known journalist) on the 31st July, 1892, and published in the *Figaro* on the 3rd August. There can

Private library of Leo XIII.

be no doubt about this interview. It was applied for in the following letter, dated 9th July, addressed to Cardinal Rampolla, and couched in sufficiently explicit language to fully enlighten the Secretary of State and the Pope on the nature and object of the desired audience, and the qualifications of the person who asked for it :—

"MONSIGNOR,

"I venture to solicit, through you, a private audience of his Holiness.

"My name will tell you who I am. It is that of a servant of the poor according to your law; of a woman who was a Christian, and remembers it to love the humble and defend the weak ; of a Socialist who, though not in a state of grace, has preserved intact, in spite of the bitter experiences of life, a deep respect for faith and a veneration for old age and captive sovereignty. My pen has more than once dared, in opposition to my own political party, to express an independent admiration of his Holiness' solicitude for the poor and friendless. This policy of the Vatican, so much in keeping with the spirit of Christ's teaching, so encouraging for those who dream of universal brotherhood, and so Christian in the highest acceptation of the word, has encouraged me to attempt what no Catholic has thought of doing, and to write to your Eminence. I am sent by M. Magnard, the editor of the *Figaro*, to ask his Holiness to give his opinion on a question that threatens to still further divide mankind, to sow discord and hatred amongst them, and to bring about bloodshed and fratricidal conflicts. I could wish that his Holiness would deign to explain his views on anti-Semitism, convinced as I am that after he has spoken there will no longer be a Christian to rebel against his teaching. Finally, I desire if possible to draw as good a portrait of Leo XIII in literature as my compatriot and friend Chartran has done on canvas. I earnestly beg your Eminence to use your powerful influence in my favour, and I place myself in your Eminence's hands.

"I have the honour to be, etc.,

"SÉVERINE."

The Cardinal replied :—

"*Rome*, 15th *July*, 1892.

"MADAM,

"I have received your letter of the 5th inst., and have laid its contents before the Holy Father. His Holiness will have no objection to receive you in private audience as soon as you inform him through me of your arrival, and as soon as his occupations permit him to grant your request. Will you therefore acquaint me of your arrival as soon as it takes place, and I will endeavour to facilitate your obtaining the audience which is the object of your journey. In the meantime I take this opportunity of offering you, etc.

"CARDINAL RAMPOLLA."

Séverine accordingly went to see the Pope, and she has written a delightful description of her interview, which lasted more than an hour, with the venerable Pontiff. Here is her full-length portrait of Pope Leo XIII :—

"Very pale, very upright, very thin, his person hardly visible, a little earthly clay in a covering of white cloth, the Holy Father was sitting at the end of the room in a large arm-chair, with his back to a console-table surmounted by a crucifix. The light fell full on this Latin prelate's face, strongly accentuating the details, the delicate modelling, the 'primitive' structure, in the pictorial meaning of the word. The face was vivified, animated, galvanized, so to speak, by a youthful mind, so combative for good, so fully alive to moral wretchedness, so full of pity for physical distress, that the glance seems like a miraculous dawn following the decline of day. Chartran's wonderful portrait alone can give an idea of the Pope's keen expression, but the flaming purple placed behind the snowy cassock throws a colour into the cheeks and a light into the eyes which they do not in reality possess. The Pope appeared to me 'whiter' than he was painted. He was more human and more touching; less of a sovereign, more of an apostle, and almost a grandfather! A tender, timid kindliness seems to lurk between his lips and peep out when he smiles; but the long firm nose reveals will, inflexible will, *the will that can wait!* Leo XIII resembles Perugino's models and the portraits in ancient religious pictures and cathedral windows: kneeling figures in profile, wearing the coarse woollen garments of humility, and praying with clasped, uplifted hands amongst apotheoses, nativities, triumphant saints, and celestial rejoicings. The Pope appeared to me like an incarnation of his family arms. His form is as slender and stately as the pine standing out against the ground azure of the Pecci blazon. His eyes are clear and bright as the morning star that shines at the summit of his heraldic tree.

"One feature of the Pope's personality attracts and retains attention almost as strongly as his face. I refer to the long, delicate, diaphanous, beautifully chiselled hands. With their agate-like nails, they remind one of precious ivory ex-votos, taken out of their case for some special occasion.

"The voice sounds far off, exiled by prayer, and more accustomed to rise towards heaven than descend to us. Nevertheless, in conversation, it comes back to earth from time to time, and breaks its Gregorian recitative with something like a major intonation.

"The Pope expresses himself both elegantly and correctly in French, with just a touch of his own nationality to flavour his remarks. The characteristic Italian exclamation, *Ecco !* 'There!') recurs constantly, like the snap of a whip, to stimulate or change the conversation."

The following passage of the interview seems to have

lost none of its *actualité* in spite of the seven years which have elapsed since it was written :—

"I spoke of Jesus pardoning His executioners, and putting forward their ignorance in excuse for their brutality; and I asked if it were not the Christian's duty to follow this example before all things.

"'Christ,' replied the Pope, 'shed His blood for all men without exception, and especially for those who stood in greater need of ransom because they believed not on Him, and obstinately adhered to their unbelief. He has bequeathed the Church a duty towards these men—the duty of bringing them back to the truth.'

"'By persuasion or persecution, Holy Father?'

"'By persuasion,' replied the Pontiff quickly. 'The Church's work can only be accomplished in gentleness and fraternity. She must endeavour to root out error, but all personal violence is contrary to the will of God and to His teaching, as well as to the character of my office and the power I wield.'

"'Then religious wars——'

"'Those two words are in contradiction,' replied the Pope, with an emphatic gesture.

"'And racial wars, Holy Father?'

"'What races? They are all sons of Adam, whom God created. What does it matter if human beings in different latitudes differ in colour and aspect? Their souls are all moulded with the same spiritual substance. Why do we send missionaries to heretics and savages? Because all human beings without exception are God's creatures. The

only difference is that some are fortunate enough to know
the true faith, and others are not. They are all equal in
the sight of the Lord, because the existence of them all is the
outcome of His will.' "

Cardinal Rampolla read and approved Séverine's article
before it appeared in print. We can easily imagine the
reception given to it by those little coteries and pontiffs who
cannot regard the Pope in any other light than that of their
Grand Almoner. Those who could not make the Pope's
views fit in with their particular tenets declared the interview apocryphal. But Séverine, as we have seen, had taken
her precautions, and once more sarcasms and insults were
hurled in vain against the walls of the Vatican.

Choir of the Sistine Chapel.

CHAPTER VII

THE POPE AS WRITER AND POET

Political, social, and doctrinal encyclicals—The Pope's favourite authors—His amusements—An ode to Christian France—Carmina Novissima—A charade-writing Pontiff.

THE written works of Leo XIII will, I think, survive intact, because they owe their existence not only to a great Pope but to a great writer. There is one part of these works especially likely to endure, because it is connected with the perennial life of the Church. I refer to the encyclicals, those declarations of the Sovereign Pontiff's masterly doctrine, in which he adheres with the perseverance of genius to the principles he had laid down for himself as early as April 1878.

" The world," he then wrote, in a letter to the bishops, " is in a state of great unrest, in regard to doctrine, social intercourse, and State government. But," he added, " God has made nations curable, and as He founded the Church for the salvation of His people, and promised to grant her His help unto the end of time, we are fully confident that the human race will be warned by the evils and calamities that oppress it, and will finally seek salvation in submission to the Church and the infallible authority of the Apostolic See."

199

Of all the Pope's encyclicals, those devoted to political
questions are the most important and numerous. We cannot
do better than quote those respectively dealing with the origin
of civil power (June 29, 1881), the religious question in
France (Feb. 8, 1884), and the Christian constitution of
states (Nov. 1, 1885), with its remarkable views on the spirit
of tolerance and liberty. The *Libertas* Constitution, in which
liberty of conscience, liberty of religion, and liberty of the
Press are defined with an incomparable loftiness of view,
should also be mentioned, as well as the 1892 encyclical to
the French people, to which we have already referred.

The social question, big as it is with coming storms,
attracts quite as much of the Pope's attention as the political
outlook. If his utterances on the former have been less frequent than on the latter, the reason is to be found in the fact
that he has encountered opposition of only a half-hearted
character in regard to social questions. His masterly *Rerum
novarum* encyclical, in which he clearly lays down the reciprocal obligations of employers and employed, has rightly
earned him the title of the Workmen's Pope—the workmen's,
not the socialists', those far from disinterested labour advo-
cates whom he denounced with the utmost vigour in his
encyclical of the 28th December, 1878, on modern errors.
A similar motive dictated the encyclical of the 20th April,
1884, in which the Pope stigmatized Masonic sects as enemies
of the Church and the public weal.

In Leo XIII the philosopher is quite as prominent as the
politician, the theologian, or the sociologist. His encyclical on
Christian philosophy (August 4, 1879) was the signal for

quite a series of reforms in the theological studies in the seminaries. Thanks to him, the young clergy are now better acquainted with the great works of the doctors of the Church, and especially St. Thomas Aquinas. We have already noticed the marked preference and deep admiration, amounting almost to adoration, expressed by Leo XIII for the Angelic Doctor, and it is interesting to observe how the Pope's energetic efforts have brought his clergy throughout the world to share his views on the matter. Mgr. d'Hulst, who was accused, wrongly as it turned out, of having taught a philosophy other than that of St. Thomas Aquinas, at the Catholic Institute in Paris, was obliged to go all the way to Rome, and produce the copy-books to convince the Pope that the charge was unfounded.

I should also mention the Pope's admirable letter on Christian marriage (Feb. 10, 1880), and what I may call his encyclicals on the mysteries of religion, such as that of the 3rd December, 1880, on the propagation of the faith, the childhood of Christ, and the schools in the East; that of the 8th June, 1883, on the Order of St. Francis; those of 1879, 1881, and 1885, conveying the good news of the Jubilee; those on the study of the Scriptures and the use of the rosary; and finally, the encyclical in which he called upon all the churches to fulfil the prophecies by uniting under the crozier of the supreme Bishop. Never before the time of Leo XIII had the Papal encyclicals had so many readers, and never have they been so much appreciated by the literati. The fact is, that the Pope's letters are not only faultless in style, but are marvellously well

adapted to the needs and anxieties of the present day.   His
compositions have the conciseness of Tacitus, the richness
and elegance of Cicero, and the grace of Sallust—the three
classical prose authors whom the Pope prizes above all others

Leo XIII at the time of his accession.

and is never tired of reading.   At the same time, his affinity
to Tacitus, Cicero, and Sallust does not prevent him from
having a marked literary individuality of his own.   As M.
Georges Goyau says :—" The Pope has accomplished the
almost impossible feat of writing with a style of his own

Leo XIII in his study (1898).

in a dead language. He does not merely translate his compositions into Latin ; he is a Latin author. This miracle was begun during his early education, and was completed after his accession to the Pontifical throne. Before that time he had all the classical scholar's knowledge and faultless elegance. Latin, however, remains a dead language to the scholar, no matter how great his attainments. It lends itself to all sorts of curious displays, mental gymnastics and dilettantism, but it is none the less dead. When he became Pope, Leo XIII took up his abode in the only spot in the world in which Latin is still a living language. Everywhere else it is more and more disregarded and allowed to fall into disuse, but the Holy See is prolonging the existence of Latin from age to age. Its history makes it the language of a governing power. It conquered and civilized the world. For several centuries it furthered the world-wide ambitions of Pagan Rome—ambitions inherited by the Christian .Church to all eternity. When Leo XIII, the depositary of these ambitions, expresses them in what may be called their native language, they inspire him with prodigies; he thinks and sees in Latin. Resolve an encyclical of Leo XIII into its component parts, and though you preserve the meaning, the inspiration has gone; it seems as if half the Papal signature at the bottom had faded away. The Pope's ample periods and vigorous assertion will not bear interference without losing their essential qualities. His secretaries have little to do with the form in which his thoughts are given to the world." It might be added, that when the Pope has signed an encyclical it is never published forthwith. The manuscript always remains several weeks in a locked drawer, the key of which the Pope keeps. There it must wait until the Holy Father, after having carefully read it over and

Cardinal Rampolla.

replaced it on the loom, as Boileau would say, at length considers it ready for the printer.

In addition to the Pope's doctrinal writings, his poetry calls for notice here. Poetry, as we have seen, was his favourite pastime as far back as his school days, when he used to write to his parents in verse, and compliment his masters in Latin stanzas. Not only the most imposing and solemn ceremonies, such as the centenary of the baptism of Clovis, but the trifling subjects of the charade-writer, stimulate the Pope to woo the Muse. His *Ode to Christian France*, written on the occasion of the fourteenth centenary of the baptism of Clovis, has been rendered by a Jesuit, Father Delaporte, in French verse, so closely reproducing the original as to justify inclusion here.[1]

CARMEN SÆCVLARE.

Vive le Christ
qui aime les Francs !

EN MÉMOIRE DU TRÈS HEUREUX JOUR OÙ LA NATION DES FRANCS
À LA SUITE DE CLOVIS SE DONNA AU CHRIST.

Les peuples ici-bas s'agitent ; Dieu les mène ;
La puissance est à lui, qui la donne ou reprend ;
Il élève, il abat toute grandeur humaine,
 Comme il lui plaît : Dieu seul est grand.

---

[1] This version may be roughly rendered into English as follows :—

CARMEN SÆCULARE.

*In memory of the most happy day on which the Franks, led by
Clovis, gave themselves to Christ.*

The peoples of this earth arise, inspired
By God, who power gives and takes away.
All human greatness doth He make and mar
As pleaseth Him ; for He alone is great.

Les Teutons menaçaient les Francs : sous leur étreinte
Les Francs allaient fléchir ; quand vers le Roi des cieux
Clovis, en qui la foi s'éveille avec la crainte,
    Tendit les bras, leva les yeux.

"O Dieu, toi qu'à genoux Clotilde adore et prie,
Sauve-nous ; à mon tour, je proclame tes droits ;
Je te donnerai tout, mes jours et ma patrie ;
    Sauve-nous, Jésus ! et je crois."

Plus d'effroi ; les guerriers retrouvent leur courage ;
L'espérance renaît sur les fronts, dans les cœurs ;
Les Francs, comme un torrent qui roule un jour d'orage,
    Écrasent leurs sanglants vainqueurs.

Tes vœux, ô roi des Francs, le Christ les réalise ;
Triomphe ! . . . Et ta parole, ô roi, tu la tiendras ;
Va, Clovis, courbe-toi sous le joug de l'Église ;
    L'évêque, à Reims, t'ouvre ses bras.

Quels sont ces étendards dans le temple ? . . O mystère !
Près de l'autel du Christ se courbe un roi puissant ;

Before the threatening Teuton hordes, the Franks
Were giving way, when, to the King of Heaven,
Clovis, with dawning faith allied to fear,
Stretched forth his arms and raised imploring eyes.

" O Thou whom Clotilde humbly doth adore,
Save us ; Thy awful sway I meekly own.
All, all I yield ; my country and my life.
Save us, O save us, Lord, and I believe."

Fear vanishes ; the Franks take heart anew,
Hope dawns again on every brow and heart.
A foaming mountain torrent now, the Franks
O'erwhelm their bloody tyrants of the eve.

Thy cry, O Frankish king, the Lord hath heard ;
Thou triumphest, but, mindful of thy word,
Thy neck shalt thou before the Church incline ;
To holy Rheims the bishop welcomes thee.

Whose be these standards in the church ? Behold !
Before Christ's altar kneels a mighty king.

Les guerriers ont suivi le prince au baptistère ;
    Après lui, le peuple y descend.

Rome, tressaille ! et vois quelle gloire est la tienne !
O reine, ô mère, étends ton royaume en tout lieu,
Ayant reçu la foi de la France chrétienne,
    Qui devient le peuple de Dieu.

Elle est ta Fille aînée ; il faudra qu'autour d'elle
On respecte sa Mère et protège ses droits . . .
Peuple fier ! Son honneur sera d'être fidèle
    A Pierre, le premier des rois.

Regarde ses héros qui s'en vont d'âge en âge ;
Le vainqueur du farouche Astolphe ouvre leurs rangs,
Lui, gardien du Pontife et du saint apanage
    Que lui fit le glaive des Francs.

Il vient, il venge Rome ; et, deux fois, la victoire
L'accompagne au travers des Alpes. Et sa main
Délivre l'Italie, et taille un territoire
    Qu'il donne au monarque Romain.

His warriors leads he to the holy font,
And all the people follow in his train.

Tremble, O Rome, and view thy wakening might !
O Queen ! O Mother ! spread thy arms o'er all !
The faith of Christian France hast thou received :
Of France, the chosen race that is to be.

Thy eldest daughter she ; her mighty sword
Shall hold thee scatheless and protect thy rights.
Her generous sons no prouder boast shall make
Than faith in Peter, greatest king of all.

From age to age, behold, her heroes come ;
Fierce Astolph's conqueror leads the goodly throng,
Waving his sword, the sword of Frankish might,
The Pope's defender and the Holy See's.

He comes. Rome is avenged, and with his arms
Once more doth Victory cross the Alps. His sword
Italia frees and carves a kingdom out
To place beneath the Roman monarch's sway.

P

Là-bas, autres exploits, autre lutte sublime :
Les Francs ont combattu : que leur triomphe est beau !
Ils ont vengé le Christ dans les murs de Solyme,
       Et reconquis le saint Tombeau.

En un siècle de deuil, quand la France chancelle,
Dieu, qu'elle a défendu, la relève et défend ;
Dieu, pour elle, combat par Jeanne la Pucelle :
       Il la sauve, par une enfant.

Calvin brise le joug du Christ ; sa frénésie
Veut étouffer les cœurs dans ses dogmes étroits ;
La noblesse de France arrache à l'hérésie
       Le peuple et le trône des rois.

France, comme aux beaux jours de ton antique histoire,
Viens, au berceau de Reims, renaître et rajeunir ! . . .
C'est l'heure, va, célèbre encore ta victoire,
       Pour revivre un long avenir.

In distant climes the mighty fight goes on ;
A splendid triumph crowns the Frankish arms ;
Christ they avenge beneath Solyma's walls,
And snatch the holy Tomb from Moslem hands.

For France a day of mourning comes, but God,
Whom she has aided, stretcheth forth His arm
And aideth her ; He sendeth Joan the Maid
And saveth France through her, a simple child.

The frantic Calvin breaks the yoke of Christ
And stifles faith within his narrow creed,
But France's nobles save from heresy
Their country and the sceptre of their kings.

O France, as in the days of long ago,
Come to the cradle of thy faith ; be born
Again ; rise from thy ashes with a shout
Of victory, and live for ever great.

Mais prends garde ! En ton ciel des nuages funèbres
Vont obscurcir l'éclat et l'honneur de ton front ;
L'erreur pèse sur toi ; prends garde ! ou ses ténèbres
     Sur tant de gloires s'étendront.

Que le Christ soit toujours ton roi ! Que dans les âmes
Il éteigne la haine aux criminels efforts !
Plus d'esclave enchaîné dans les sectes infâmes !
     Soyez unis ; vous serez forts.

La vie, elle est en toi ; qu'elle se renouvelle !
Les siècles ont passé, mais ton cœur est vivant.
Courez, fils de la France, aux rives de la Vesle [1]
     Pour marcher ensemble en avant.

Aux échos d'Orient ton nom résonne, ô France ;
Va, sur ces bords lointains que ton pas ébranla,
Avec la foi du Christ, porter la délivrance,
     Plante la croix et défends-la.

But have a care ; behold the threatening clouds
That gather o'er thy head. Alas, they seek
To mask thy brow with error. O beware,
And let thy glorious past unsullied shine !

Let Christ remain thy king ! Let every soul
Be open to His word ; let hatred cease,
Let Sect give up its captives, let the world
Behold your union and the strength it gives.

Though centuries have passed, thy heart is still
A spring of life : let life well up again
As in the past. O valiant sons of France,
To Vesla's banks press on, and onward still.

Thy name resounds, O France, on Orient's shore.
The path that shook beneath thy feet O seek
Again, and let thy hand set up the cross
Of Christ, and bear salvation unto all.

[1] The river on which Rheims, the ancient cradle of the Christian faith in France, stands.

Avec la foi du Christ, tout vit, grandit, prospère ;
Sans elle tout languit et meurt. . . .   Va ton chemin ;
Toi qui fus, par le Christ, si grande, ô France, espère !
Tu le seras encore demain.

A collection of the Pope's poetry has lately been published,
under the title of *Carmina Novissima*, with a preface by

Leo XIII and the Pontifical Court.

Father Enrico Vallé, of the Society of Jesus.   His Holiness'
poetry is, Father Vallé considers, distinctly Virgilian, not only
in the arrangement of sentences, which is more a matter of

Without the faith of Christ can nothing thrive,
But in that faith is power and life.   And thou,
O France, who once through Christ wast great, mayst hope,
And greatness shall thy portion be again. —Trans.

style than poetical temperament, but in its elevated conception, its selection and division of ideas, and graceful ease of expression. It has, moreover, the gentle but majestic movement of the Virgilian period.   Virgil is, in fact, the Pope's favourite among

Cardinal Vincenzo Vannutelli.

all the Latin poets.   It would of course be impracticable to make copious quotations from the Pope's poetical works here, but the following exhortation, addressed by the Pope to a young spendthrift of noble family, whose name he disguises under that of Florus, merits attention :—

AD FLORUM (1883).[1]

Flore puer, vesana diu te febris adurit :
     Inficit immundo mollia membra situ
Dira lues ; cupidis stygio respersa veneno,
     Nec pudor est, labiis pocula plena bibis.
l'ocula sunt Circes : apparent ora ferarum ;
     Vel canis immundus, sus vel amica luto.
Si sapis, ô tandem, miser, expergiscere, tandem,
     Ulla tuæ si te cura salutis habet,
Heu fuge Sirenum cantus, fuge litus avarum. . . .

Here is " Leo's last prayer " :—

DEO ET VIRGINI MATRI.[2]

Extrema Leonis Vota.

Extremum radiat, pallenti involvitur umbra
     Jam jam sol moriens : nox subit atra, LEO,
Atra tibi : arescunt venæ, nec vividus humor
     Perfluit ; exhausto corpore vita perit.
Mors telum fatale jacit ; velamine amicta
     Funereo, gelidus contegit ossa lapis.
Aet anima aufugiens excussis libera vinclis,
     Continuo ætherias ardet anhela plagas ;

---

[1] Florus, my child, a fierce fever hath long consumed thee ; a cruel plague infects thy nerveless limbs with filthy rottenness ; with eager lips thou, shameless, drinkest from cups filled with an infernal poison. These cups are Circe's ; on them are the figures of beasts, the unclean dog, and the swine wallowing in mud. If thou art wise, O wretched one, awake ; if thou hast any care for thy salvation, shun the syrens' song and the all-devouring shore.

[2] TO GOD AND THE VIRGIN MOTHER.

Leo's Last Prayer.

After a final gleam, the Sun pales, clothes itself in shadow, and, dying, downward sinks ; black night descends, O Leo.

Huc celerat cursum ; longarum hæc meta viarum ;
Expleat oh clemens anxia vota Deus !
Oh cælum attingam ! supremo munere detur
Divino æternum lumine et ore frui.
Teque, o Virgo, frui ; matrem te parvulus infans
Dilexi, flagrans in sene crevit amor.
Excipe me cælo ; cæli de civibus unus
Auspice te, dicam, prœmia tanta tuli.

As a final quotation we may read these two stanzas, composed in 1885, in which the poet reminds his readers of the promise of immortality by Christ to His Church : [1]—

Occidit—inclamant—solio dejectus, in ipso
Carcere, in ærumnis occidit ecce Leo.
Spes insana : Leo alter adest, qui sacra volentes
Jura dat in populos, imperium que tenet.

But Leo XIII does not disdain purely secular literature.

It seizes thee ; no more the generous blood courses through thy dried-up veins ; life flees thy exhausted body.

Death throws his fatal dart ; thy bones, enveloped in the funeral shroud, shall lie imprisoned beneath the cold stone.

But the soul, released from bondage, soars up to Heaven, the object of its hopes.

The soul hastens ; the end of its long journeying is at hand. O merciful God ! hear its anguished cry !

May I reach Heaven, and, O last boon of all, delight for ever in the divine light and presence of my God.

And be with thee, O Virgin, whom I, a little child, loved as a mother, and now, an aged man, cherish still more ardently.

Receive me into Heaven, and I, a fellow-citizen of the saints, will attribute so splendid a reward to thee.

[1] Hurled from his throne, they cry, Leo expires wretchedly in a dungeon. Vain hope ; another Leo succeeds him, gives laws unto the people, and holds sway.

He is a regular contributor to the *Vox Urbis*, a recently established Roman magazine, written entirely in Latin. Under the heading "Ænigmata," this magazine has published charades written by no less a person than Leo XIII. A charade-writing Pope! Another opportunity for the Pharisees!

CHAPTER VIII

THE POPE AND THE AMERICAN MOVEMENT

Progress of Roman Catholicism in the United States—The Knights of Labour—Cardinal Gibbons in Rome—Church and State—Mgr. Ireland—The Apostolic delegate and the University of Washington—The recall of Mgr. Keane—Mgr. Schrœder's intrigues—His exclusion—The *Life of Father Hecker*—Story of an imprimatur—The Pope's letter on the American movement.

IN America there are not, and cannot be, any relations between Church and State. The constitution of the United States says :—" Congress shall pass no law either establishing a State religion or interfering with the free profession of religion." Under these circumstances, it is curious that during the nineteenth century no people should have given more marked signs of what Cardinal Gibbons calls the " power of attraction" of the Romish Church. M. Brunetière does not hesitate to describe the progress of Roman Catholicism in the United States as miraculous. M. Paul Bourget was struck by the same fact before it attracted M. Brunetière's attention, and the author of *Outre Mer* has given eloquent expression to his surprise and pleasure. Moreover, there is no disputing the evidence of correct statistics. One hundred and twenty-five years ago, out of a population of three millions, there were

only thirty or forty thousand Catholics—barely one per cent.
—one Episcopal see, and ten churches. To-day, out of a population of sixty-five millions, there are ten million Catholics,
or more than one-seventh of the total; there are eighty-eight
episcopal sees, eight thousand priests, and six thousand
churches. New York is the most important Roman Catholic
city in the world, after Paris and Vienna.

It would have been impossible for Leo XIII not to feel
the greatest interest in this religious evolution, which is calculated to attract the attention of any serious mind. It
would have been equally impossible for theologians of the
old school, brought up in the respect of traditions, not to feel
uneasy at the rapid growth of the Church amongst a system
of liberty of which they are accustomed to see only the most
dangerous side. Again, the use of an almost boundless
liberty could not but involve at least some abuses; and this
is exactly what has happened. If we study the history of
the American Church during the last few years, we see the
Pope's well-meant efforts constantly thwarted by malevo-
lent opposition, until at length the Pope was obliged to condemn, under the name of Americanism, doctrines which were
never professed by the American episcopate, but which had
nevertheless made a certain number of converts in the United
States and elsewhere. By this condemnation, which his
opponents immediately hailed as a victory for themselves,
Leo XIII has really rendered the American Church the
greatest possible service. He not only pointed out great
dangers against which she will henceforth be able to better
defend herself, but, by clearly defining unacceptable and con-

demnable doctrines and tendencies, he freed her from any
renewal of the vague and unjust attacks of which she was too
often the victim.

About ten years ago the intransigeants in the United
States flattered themselves on obtaining what they regarded
as a Papal condemnation of the Knights of Labour.   Cardinal
Gibbons, seeing that the Pope had been misled by false
reports, went to Rome and pleaded the Knights' cause.   He
pointed out that they were in no way connected with Socialism, or at least with Socialism as understood in Europe, and
that their association was founded solely with a view to the
defence of working men's interests.   I happened to see the
Cardinal on his return from Rome, and I questioned him on
the result of his journey.

"The Knights of Labour," he replied, "have now no better
friend than the Pope."

Only a short time before the Cardinal's journey to Rome,
the Pope had recognized, in his encyclical to the bishops of
the United States, that the separatist system had enabled
American Roman Catholicism to make decided progress; but
the Holy Father also declared that this system could only be
regarded as provisional, and that the true doctrine, for
America as well as other nations, consisted of the close union
of the civil and religious power.

That, the Cardinal told me, is the theory.   "The Pope was
quite right to lay it down, and I fully agree with it, but
that does not alter the fact that our present conditions of
existence are founded on an hypothesis, and the Pope is the
first to admit that this hypothesis does not in any way

interfere with the development of the American Church.
To accomplish its mission, the Church requires nothing but
liberty, because its teachings are truth, and to know truth
is to love it. Therefore, to be loved the Church requires
only to be known. We have all the liberty we need in the
United States, and although there are no official relations
between Church and State, there is between them something much better—a sort of *entente cordiale.* The State
gives us liberty, and we respect its authority—two things
which are the strongest bases of national strength. A nation
in which authority and liberty are both respected cannot but
prosper." We have reproduced this statement of the Archbishop of Baltimore's views because they show his entire
agreement with Leo XIII. The same ideas can be found
in the Pope's political encyclicals, just as most of Cardinal
Gibbons' views on social questions can be discovered in the
social encyclicals, and especially the one known as the
Rerum Novarum.

But the questions connected with the Knights of Labour,
and the relations between Church and State, were not the
only ones to which the partisans of routine directed their efforts
to prejudice the most prominent members of the American
episcopate in the eyes of the Pope. For instance, they
denounced an educational system favoured by Mgr. Ireland,
Archbishop of St. Paul, Minnesota. The basis of this system
was educational neutrality—a sincere and benevolent neutrality, quite different from the hypocritical and deceptive
attitude of which the contemporary history of the Church in
France contains only too many instances. The struggle was

a long one, and is still, perhaps, in progress, Rome not having yet made a sufficiently definite declaration to put a stop to the controversy. The reply of the Holy See could hardly, in fact, have been anything but an act of tolerance: *tolerari posse*. The Holy Father, however, had sent an apostolic delegate, Mgr. Satolli, to the United States. In the Pope's opinion, the appointment of an apostolic delegate to the United States could have no other object than that of tightening the bond of union between the American Church and the Holy See. Some of Mgr. Satolli's friends none the less relied upon him to keep watch over Mgr. Gibbons, Mgr. Ireland, and their supporters, so as to destroy the influence of these two great prelates over the University of Washington, the rector of which was then Mgr. Keane. At first Mgr. Satolli seemed destined to disappoint these secret hopes. His arrival in Washington excited little enthusiasm, because the American priesthood regarded his nomination as a proof of distrust on the part of the Holy See towards them, and because they anticipated that Mgr. Satolli's attitude would soon prove a cause of trouble. Mgr. Satolli, however, managed to make such great and visible progress in the good graces of Cardinal Gibbons and Cardinal Ireland, that he soon began to share in the personal popularity of these two prelates, especially after the very liberal speech which he delivered at Chicago on "The Gospel and the American Constitution." Mgr. Satolli's honeymoon with the American Church was not, however, of long duration. As soon as he had obtained a certain amount of authority and influence, thanks to Cardinals Gibbons and Ireland, he considered that the time had come to take action against those two prelates. In 1896, Mgr. Keane, rector of the Catholic University of Washington, was removed from his post by an order from Rome, immediately after the beginning of the term. This

Cardinal Ludochowski, head of the Propaganda.

step was directly due to the apostolic delegate's influence. Mgr. Keane submitted to the will of the Holy See. He uncomplainingly gave up the high post for which he had been chosen by his eighty colleagues, and in which he had rendered important services to the Church in the space of a few years.

In accordance with the Pope's desire, he went to Rome, and was not a little surprised to hear his Holiness, who had become better informed in the meantime, express regret at the un-

Cardinal Serafino Vannutelli.

expected measure of which the eminent rector had been the victim.   As a sort of set-off, the Holy Father appointed Mgr. Keane Archbishop of Damascus and adviser to the congregations of Studies and of the Propaganda.   This was a public recognition of Mgr. Keane's doctrinal worth and zeal for the propagation of the faith.

The dismissal of Mgr. Keane had been the result of direct representations on the part of Mgr. Satolli to the Holy See. The apostolic delegate was led to take this action, which was evidently against the wishes of the American bishops, by the intrigues of a German professor, Mgr. Schrœder. The latter, not content with the removal of Mgr. Keane, resumed his intrigues against Mgr. Conaty, the successor and friend of the former rector. This time the University patronage committee of archbishops and bishops did not give Mgr. Schrœder time to attain his object. At the request of the Senate (or council of professors) of the University, the committee removed Mgr. Schrœder from his post. A very extraordinary thing followed. A despatch from Rome ordered the committee to reinstate the unworthy professor. This despatch was addressed to Mgr. Martinelli, who, in the meantime, had succeeded Mgr. Satolli. It was communicated by Mgr. Martinelli to Cardinal Gibbons, who in turn officially laid it before the committee of bishops. It created a painful sensation, and set up a resistance the gravity of which it was impossible to mistake. Cardinal Gibbons telegraphed to the Pope that as the decision taken against Mgr. Schrœder had been duly placed on record, it seemed impossible to reverse it. The Cardinal added that he was sending a full explanatory statement of the case. The Pope read the statement with the attention it deserved, and ordered that the matter should be settled "in accordance with the wishes of the bishops."

Mgr. Satolli's friends were beaten, but they were not long in obtaining their revenge. In April 1898, the Abbé Klein, one of the most distinguished professors at the Catholic Institute in Paris, published a French translation of the *Life of Father Hecker*, founder of the Paulist order, by Father Elliott, a member of that order. The translation was accompanied by a preface by Abbé Klein, an introduction by Mgr. Ireland, and a letter from Cardinal Gibbons, all couched in a strain of great admiration for the author and the hero of the book. Mgr. Satolli's friends immediately set to work to have the work placed on the *Index Expurgatorius*. Such a condemnation would, they thought, involve that of not only the book but its author, translator, and apologists. It would further, they considered, deal a heavy blow at what it pleased them to describe as Americanism, Father Hecker being venerated by the American Church as one of its best representatives. Cardinal Gibbons had not only expressed this feeling of veneration, but he had set out its origin in the following letter, which appears in the sixth edition of M. Klein's translation :—

> *"Baltimore Cathedral, Maryland.*
> *"April* 14, 1898.

"MY DEAR FATHER ELLIOTT,

"It gives me great satisfaction to declare my opinion of Father Hecker and to have it made known. Father Hecker was undoubtedly an instrument of Providence for the diffusion of the Catholic faith in our country. He did a great deal of good in bringing non-Catholics nearer to us, in lessening prejudice, and in gaining the ear of the public for our religion, without counting the multitude of those who owe their conversion directly or indirectly to him. His mind was that of a child in submission to the Holy Church. It was a Catholic mind in the

Q

fullest meaning of the word. His life was adorned by every fruit of
personal piety. He was animated by truly apostolic zeal for the
salvation of souls—a zeal which was always bold but at the same time
prudent, so as to attract Protestants without the smallest sacrifice of
orthodoxy. Divine Providence gave him the help of a community of
men inspired by as lofty motives as his own. The Paulists are
continuing the work to which he devoted his life, the conversion of
souls to the Catholic faith, and, by the grace of God, they have had
marvellous success. The special services they have held in their church
in New York city have given proof of this success by the very large
number of sinners who have been brought to repentance and of
Protestants who have been converted, instructed, and baptized. They
have, moreover, conducted services and meetings for non-Catholics all
over the United States. Their congregations are frequently composed
exclusively of Protestants. They have, further, greatly extended
Father Hecker's organization for the distribution of Catholic literature.
The Paulists have shown themselves equal to great apostolic enterprises.
They have always displayed unreserved respect and obedience to the
ecclesiastical authorities. I learn with pleasure that Father Hecker's
career is becoming more and more appreciated in Europe since his
life and writings have been made known there.

" Wishing you the holy joys of the Easter season,

"I am,

"Yours most faithfully,

"J. CARDINAL GIBBONS."

It was clear to the opposition that if they could obtain
the official condemnation of the *Life of Father Hecker*
they would be striking at the heads of the American Church.
A French priest, the Abbé Maignen, who had formerly been
censured by the Archbishop of Paris for a scurrilous attack
on the Comte de Mun, undertook to carry on the campaign.
He drew up a violent and unfair pamphlet entitled "Is
Father Hecker a saint?" This pamphlet, which first appeared
in instalments in the *Vérité*, and was afterwards published

separately, represented Cardinals Gibbons and Ireland and other eminent leaders of the American Church as the accomplices of rebellious priests such as M. Charbonnel and M. Bourrier. It further spoke of "campaigns" carried on against the authority of the Holy See, and "an American syndicate formed to float an American saint in Europe." The venerable Cardinal Richard, after consulting those best qualified to advise him, refused to grant his imprimatur to this pamphlet. The Abbé Maignen and his friends promptly appealed to Rome, confident as they were that the accomplices they needed would be found in the Holy Father's *entourage.* The imprimatur refused by Cardinal Richard was given at once by Mgr. Lepidi, master of the sacred apostolic palaces. Mgr. Keane was obliged to complain to Cardinal Rampolla, who had no difficulty in showing that neither he nor the Holy Father was responsible. "The Pope and I knew nothing about it," he said. Mgr. Ireland also protested, but he was unable to prevent the publication of an English edition of the pamphlet, with Mgr. Lepidi's imprimatur. Cardinal Gibbons considered the matter sufficiently serious to lay before the Council of Archbishops, and Father Elliott was asked to draw up a report. The affair was at this stage when it was learnt that the Pope, uninfluenced by the efforts to make a breach between him and the American prelates, had removed the case from the jurisdiction of the Roman congregations in order to deal with it himself, in accordance with his right. The result was that the *Life of Father Hecker* was not placed on the Index, and the Pope wrote Cardinal Gibbons a masterly letter, in which he condemned

what ought to be condemned in the doctrines held by or
attributed to Father Hecker, as well as in the doctrines
propagated under the name of Americanism by the enemies
of Cardinals Gibbons and Ireland.

Cardinal Parocchi.

The Pope's letter, after expressing admiration and
sympathy for the work of the Cardinal and his colleagues,
and for the genius of the American people, " always ready to
promote noble enterprises and to seek for whatever may

conduce to the progress of civilization and the prosperity of the country," refers as follows to the new opinions constituting the chief object of the Papal letter :—

Cardinal Gotti.

"The theory on which these new opinions are based is, broadly, that, in order to more easily bring back dissentients to Catholic truth, the Church ought to draw nearer to a full-grown civilization, relax her former vigour, and show

herself conciliatory to the aspirations and requirements of
modern communities. This principle, however, is extended
by many not only to discipline but to doctrines connected
with the custody of the faith. They assert that it is advis-
able, for the sake of bringing back those who have strayed
from the fold, to ignore or to close our eyes to certain
doctrinal declarations, regarded as of minor importance, and
to carry out this line of conduct to such an extent as to no
longer give these declarations the meaning always attributed
to them by the Church. It needs no long dissertation to
show how entirely this design must be disapproved." With
regard to discipline, the Pope goes on—" It is only just that
the Apostolic See should take into account the customs and
requirements of so many different peoples, but private
individuals, who may be too easily led away by what they
consider the right course to pursue, cannot be allowed to
settle the question. This is the province of the Church."
The Pope then goes on to condemn, as contrary to doctrine
and discipline, the contention that "a certain amount of
liberty should be introduced into the Church, so that the
consequent diminution of the power and vigilance of the
central authority would leave every individual Catholic more
free to develop his own initiative and personal resources."
The Pope declines to admit "the rejection of all external
authority as superfluous and even comparatively useless to
those who strive after Christian perfection" under pretext
that the Holy Spirit "now blesses the faithful with more
abundant spiritual gifts than in the past." His Holiness
declaims against "those lovers of novelty who attach more

than the needful importance to natural virtues, as if those
virtues were better adapted to the ways and the needs of our
times, and as if their possession were in proportion to the
amount of activity and energy they excite." He rejects the
illusory distinction between active and passive virtues, as well
as the rash assertion that "the religious life is of little or no
use to the Church." The Pope concludes thus :—

"From what We have said, it will be evident that We
cannot approve the opinions which have been designated in
various quarters as constituting what is called Americanism.
If this word is intended to cover certain intellectual gifts
which are an honour to the American nation, just as other
gifts are an honour to other nations, or if the word signifies
the constitution of your states and the laws and customs in
force among you, there is assuredly nothing in Americanism
which could lead Us to reject it ; but if the word is employed
not only to designate the doctrines mentioned above, but to
accentuate them, can it be doubted that Our venerable
Brethren the American Bishops would be the very first to
reject it and to condemn it as an insult to themselves and
their nation ? "

And the Pope ends, as he began, with a declaration of
benevolence and affection :—

"We extend the blessing of God over all your nation,
which has not only done much for religion in the past,
but promises to do still more in the future. We lovingly
bestow on you and all the faithful in America Our apostolic
benediction, an earnest of Divine favour."

Mgr. Ireland had no difficulty in joining in the Papal

condemnation of doctrines which were falsely attributed to
him but were never his. Father Elliott and the Paulists
followed Mgr. Ireland's example, and the Abbé Klein
voluntarily withdrew his book from circulation.

"What would you do," one of the princes of the Church

Cardinal Svampa.

was asked, "if the Holy See tried to force you to admit that
two and two make six?"

"I would admit it at once," was the reply; "and before
signing I would ask, 'Wouldn't you like me to make it
seven?'"

There is no such ironical reservation in the acceptance

of the Pope's letter by Cardinal Gibbons and his three colleagues, who have invariably set a much better example of complete and filial submission to the Holy See than some of their adversaries have done. I am, moreover, inclined to think that the Pope's letter to Cardinal Gibbons will trouble

Cardinal Ireland.

the enemies of the American Church more than its friends. Leo XIII has pulled down part of the house to preserve the rest from fire, while the enemies to whom I refer seem to have desired the destruction of the entire edifice. The Pope has come to the rescue again, and has unmistakably saved the situation.

CHAPTER IX

THE FUTURE POPE

Probable successors—The vanity of prognostication—A long-lived Pope—The prophecies of St. Malachi.

IT is said that when Cardinal Franchi, the present Pope's first Secretary of State, was warmly congratulated on his appointment, he replied—

"You need not be in such a hurry. Who knows how long I shall keep my post? The new Pope is so old! He will not reign three years."

Four months after this conversation Cardinal Franchi died suddenly. Leo XIII has since outlived nearly all the cardinals who were regarded as *papabili* for the future Conclave, so that the prophets are constantly finding themselves obliged to prophesy anew, and seem to be condemned to something like the labour of Penelope. At present Cardinal Oreglia seems to be the favourite. He is camerlengo and senior member of the Sacred College. In this double capacity he would at once exercise considerable power on the Holy See becoming vacant. It is said that Cardinal Gotti, of the Carmelite order, will be the candidate of the Triple Alliance, failing Cardinal Serafino Vannutelli, whose candida-

234

ture was previously too pronounced to leave him much
prospect of success, and Cardinal Vincenzo Vannutelli, who
will wisely confine himself to "making the running" for his
brother. Neither Cardinal Parocchi nor Cardinal Rampolla
can hope to wear the tiara; the one because his duties as
Cardinal Vicar have necessarily created a good deal of
dissatisfaction against him among the Italian prelates, who
form the majority in the Sacred College, and the other
because, as Secretary of State to Leo XIII, he is closely
identified with the present order of things, and would therefore not be able to undertake the government of the Church
with entire freedom of action or mind. France is waiting
until the opportunity arises for her to take an active interest
in the question, but I believe the Government and the French
cardinals would not object to the election of Cardinal
Capecelatro, who is supposed to have liberal ideas, and that
they would hail with pleasure the election of Cardinal
Svampa, Archbishop of Bologna, who has a great love for
France, and would adhere, it may at least be hoped, to the
traditions of Leo XIII. One objection to Cardinal Svampa
is his age. Born in 1851, he is the youngest member of the
Sacred College, and his accession would be likely to mean
too long a reign to please the electors, who are themselves
eligible. He does, however, appear to be designated for the
office by the prophecies of the Irish Saint Malachi. This
may not amount to a great deal, but I am acquainted with
a considerable number of people who attach considerable
importance to these perhaps apocryphal prophecies, which I
may mention here without guaranteeing their authenticity.

Many of them, moreover, might be applied to almost any Pope, and some are so obscure as to defy analysis. For instance, Clement XI is referred to as *flores circumdati*. That does not commit the prophet to much. Clement XI expressed himself in elaborate language, which enabled the prophet's believers to explain—after the event—that *flores circumdati* meant flowers of rhetoric. Innocent XIII is spoken of as *de bona religione*. No doubt, but the religion of other Popes was as good as his. Benedict XIII is *miles in bello*. Possibly he was more militant than other Popes, but all of them have made war against the errors of their times. In regard to Clement XII—*columna excelsa*—the prophecy is still far from explicit. All Popes are highly placed, and there is nothing to prevent any one of them from being compared to a column, as they all support the Church which the Divine Founder Himself likened to a house. Benedict XIV has a curious epithet—*animal rurale*—applied to him. He was, it is true, born in the country, but he was certainly not the only Pope so born. Then we come to something better. Clement XIII is *rosa umbria*. He came from Venice, where this kind of rose is very abundant. The application of the saying is of course evident. Clement XIV is *visus velox vel ursus velox*. I give this up. The prophecy is a little more precise in regard to Pius VI—*peregrinus apostolicus*. Certainly few Popes accomplished such pilgrimages as Pius VI, who was driven out of Rome, and ended his days at Valence. But how are we to explain the description of Pius VII as *aquila rapax*? Pius VII had not always reason to be pleased with his dealings with the Imperial eagle, but the prophecy refers to the Pope and not to Napoleon. The prophet further describes Leo XII as *canis et columba*, Pius VIII as *vir religiosus*, Gregory XVI as *de balneis Etrurial*, Pius IX as *crux de cruce*, Leo XIII as *lumen in cœlo*, and his successors in the following order :—*ignis ardens, religio depopulata, fides intrepida, pastor angelicus*, and *pastor et nauta.*

According to this prophecy, or pseudo-prophecy, there will be only five Popes after Leo XIII. During the last reign the Church will be exposed to terrible persecutions :—" The Roman Pontiff shall feed his flock in many tribulations ; and then at the appointed time the city on the seven hills shall be destroyed, and the dread Judge shall judge the people."

It may be observed in conclusion, that the predictions concerning the five successors of Leo XIII apply quite as well to him as do the words referring specially to himself. If his genius can be compared to a shining light in heaven—*lumen in cœlo*—do not his persevering efforts to bring back the dissentient Churches within the fold bear witness to a truly apostolic zeal and ardour—*ignis ardens?* And cannot it be said that during his reign religion has been attacked and invaded on all sides—*religio depopulata?* Finally, who can cast a doubt on the faith of this pastor and pilot—*fides intrepida, pastor angelicus, pastor et nauta?* Clearly, prophecies as to future Popes can only be accepted with caution, and there is nothing to prove that we are so close to the valley of Jehoshaphat.

THE END